Bound

Book I in the Danport Series

Renée Hill

Quill Hawk Publishing

Copyright © 2026 by Renée Hill

All rights reserved. No part of this book may be used or reproduced in any manner whatsoever, including the purpose of training artificial intelligence technologies under Article 4(3) of the Digital Single Market Directive 2019/790; Quill Hawk Publishing and the author(s) expressly reserves this work from the text and data mining exception. Only brief quotations embodied in critical articles or reviews may be allowed.

Cover designed by Lil Lady Marketing & Design

Manufactured in the United States

ISBN 978-1-965142-86-8 (paperback)

ISBN 978-1-965142-87-5 (hardback)

Library of Congress Control Number: 2026900823

Quill Hawk Publishing
Edmond, Oklahoma

Contents

Dedication	VII
Prologue	VIII
1. THE PREMONITION	1
2. POWERS AND RULERS OF DARKNESS	4
3. A VIRTUOUS WOMAN, WHO CAN FIND?	6
4. CHOSEN	8
5. WHITEWASHED SEPULCHRES	12
6. WHEN THOU PRAYEST	15
7. FIRST THINGS FIRST	18
8. MISSION STATEMENT: KILL, STEAL, AND DESTROY	20
9. TALEBEARER	22
10. SPIRITS OF DEVILS	25
11. THE SABBATH	32
12. EMBRACE THE CHAOS	38
13. HUSBANDS, LOVE YOUR WIVES	40

14. EL ROI: GOD WHO SEES ME	42
15. PURE IN HEART	45
16. TAKE ME OUT TO THE BALLPARK	47
17. LOVE ONE ANOTHER	49
18. ONE LOAF AT A TIME	51
19. HOUSE TO HOUSE	55
20. TWO OR THREE	58
21. FOLLY	60
22. WRETCHED	64
23. THE INTERESTS OF OTHERS	67
24. STIRRING THE POT	69
25. EXHORT ONE ANOTHER	71
26. COUNSEL	74
27. SCHOOL DAYS	76
28. TATTLERS	80
29. IRON SHARPENS	83
30. FRIDAY NIGHT LIGHTS	86
31. DATE NIGHT	88
32. DEADLY ARROWS	92
33. MY FLESH AND MY HEART FAILETH	93
34. IT ONLY TAKES A SPARK	97
35. BATTLES	99

36.	REACHING OUT	101
37.	SUNDAY	103
38.	CAN'T TRUST THAT DAY	106
39.	SEE YOU AT THE POLE	114
40.	COMMONALITY	116
41.	SURVIVING THE NIGHT	118
42.	WITH A LITTLE HELP FROM FRIENDS	122
43.	FOR THIS CHILD	129
44.	STEPS OF A GOOD MAN	133
45.	SHARE WITH OTHERS	139
46.	SONS	146
47.	EXPOSED	153
48.	HONOR YOUR PASTOR	160
49.	BEFORE IT IS EASY	168
50.	OLD THINGS ARE PASSED AWAY	173
51.	TRUTH	177
52.	MONSTERS ARE REAL	181
53.	SILENT NIGHT	189
54.	CAMPING	191
55.	ILLUMINATION	194
56.	THE WOOD FAIRY	196
57.	ALL FALL SHORT	198

58.	YOU NEVER KNOW	201
59.	TOO MANY CHIEFS	203
60.	THE MEETING	206
61.	RELENTLESS	210
62.	SET FREE	216
63.	GIFT FROM GOD	218
64.	WEAPONS OF WARFARE	220
65.	STAY THE COURSE	224
Epilogue		227
Acknowledgments		230
BOUND II		232

Dedication

Over my lifetime, I've been privileged to know a few true intercessors, who, by example, taught me so much: believers, the extent of whose impact is known only to God; and saints, who wrestled against principalities, powers, the rulers of darkness, and spiritual wickedness with a fierce tenacity. While investing in eternity, these spiritual giants quietly fought the fight of faith without any interest in fame, applause, or the approval of humans. They've often had a serenity about them, a quiet confidence, as if they knew something that the rest of us simply weren't privy to, and I suspect they did.
It is to these prayer warriors, who have forever impacted my life, this book is dedicated.

Prologue

For when they shall say peace and safety: then sudden destruction cometh upon them...

1 Thessalonians 5:3-4

Lights shone warmly from the windows of the cracker box houses lining the shady streets of Danport, Vermont. The red and orange leaves of century old trees provided a hospitable canopy for the old brick paved roads, preserved because of their historical value. On one end of Main Street, the courthouse presided; and on the other end, the high steeple of the colonial style Community Church towered. This fall night was crisp as dogs called to each other from back yards, and a cat rubbed its back against one of the countless pumpkins that decorated the front porches of most homes. Steamy smoke churned out of chimneys, and the aromas of fresh baked bread, simmering stew, roast, fried chicken, and ham wafted from the kitchens of the quaint little hamlet, blending together in a beautiful potpourri of edible fragrances, causing the stranger's mouth to water and his stomach to growl.

As his dark figure walked down the sidewalk, he noticed a bicycle pulled up to the front steps of one of the homes he passed. A baseball bat leaned against its porch rail, the voices of children filled the air with chatter, until *Mom* reminded them to wash their hands and come sit down at the table announcing, "It's time for supper." The thought crossed the stranger's mind that Norman Rockwell himself could not have painted a cozier picture. If only they knew.

Dread followed him and the musty odor of layer upon layer of regret and abhorrent, heinous memories filled his heart with a murky despair. His boots clicked, clicked, clicked as he walked back toward the church. Glancing into the window of the next home he passed, he noticed the woman. He recognized her from today and remembered the empathy in her eyes and the way she'd looked at him with such concern when she saw him at the church earlier. This must be her home, her family. He stopped in his tracks, standing motionless for a moment, watching as she and her family joined hands around their dinner table and bowed their heads. The scene stirred within him longing for a distant past, but for a few smoldering cinders, almost forgotten. His eyes misted when unexpectantly, he was jarred back to reality as he felt the now familiar heavy weight of oppression suddenly weighing down on him, binding him, each arduous step heavy, like trudging through molasses, but his course was set. With difficulty, the stranger kept walking.

Chapter One
THE PREMONITION

Howbeit when He, the Spirit of truth, is come, He will guide you into all truth: for He shall not speak of Himself; but whatsoever He shall hear, that shall He speak: and He will shew you things to come.

John 16:13

Goodness, he thought, as a chill ran down his spine. Danport's local handyman Henry Griffin shivered as he noticed a shadow pass by his front window. It was the figure of a man, barely noticeable out the side of Henry's eye, and yet something inside of him did notice and was instantly on high alert. Ill at ease, he tried to shake it off, taking the hands of his wife and their oldest daughter, Jeannie, as each member of his young family bowed his or her head to bless the food his wife has managed to throw together. Sometimes he didn't know how she did it. This meal was perfect, especially considering the low budget with which she had to work. He knew raising their brood, a small tribe, on his salary couldn't be easy, and yet Ruth never complained; she just patched up another pair of well-worn jeans so she could pass them down to the next youngster in line, six to be exact. God broke the mold when he created Ruth, and Henry had no doubt he was a blessed man. Tonight's meal consisted of a green salad and burritos that Ruth made from last night's leftover pinto beans. It was all delicious; Ruth was a miracle worker. After dinner, the children carried their plates into the kitchen, rinsed and then loaded them into the dishwasher. Ruth had trained them well. "Time for baths," she announced as she poured Henry a cup of coffee. "Jeannie, you go first. The rest of you start on your homework." She sat down next to him on the couch, and they began to talk about their day. "Matthew already has the choir at church, working on the Christmas pageant. He's asked Jeannie to play the bells."

"She'll do a great job. She's so responsible that daughter of yours," Henry responded, grinning.

"Well, she has your musical talent, that daughter of yours," she chuckled in return. Her expression faded into a frown as Ruth softly said, "Henry, I saw a stranger in town today, which, of course, is no big deal, but there was something about him. I'm not sure what it was. There was a sadness in his eyes that made my heart ache, but it also made me feel a little uneasy."

"Where did you see him?"

"Well, I was in the sanctuary putting the hymnals back in place and tidying up a bit, and there he was in the doorway. I asked him if I could help him, but he didn't speak. He just looked at me. I bet he stood there frozen, saying nothing, just staring for a whole minute, which may not sound like a long time, but have you ever just watched a clock's second hand for a whole minute? It's a long time. He kinda spooked me."

"I don't like you being alone down there. So much could go wrong, Ruth, even in a church. What happened to the guy?"

"I don't know. Pastor Scott hollered for me from the hallway, and the guy turned away, kind of pathetic like, and just walked right out the front doors of the church. I've been praying for him off and on all afternoon. I don't know why, but it was sort of unsettling somehow."

"I'll speak with Pastor tomorrow at church and see if he's noticed the guy. I've got to work on the oven down there anyway."

"Okay," she said as she patted him on the thigh, "I better go check on the kids and see how homework and tonight's conveyor belt into the tub is progressing," and with that Ruth climbed the stairs.

Henry couldn't help but smile as he heard her hollering instructions at their kids like a drill sergeant. Being a mom was definitely her calling. The thing about Ruth is that she knew who she was. She'd always wanted to be a housewife and mother, so she'd found her niche, and in this she found great joy. At 5'7" she was still slim, even after having six kids. Her brunette hair was generally on top of her head or in a ponytail, and she rarely wore makeup, maybe a little eye liner and lipstick when she went out. After all, Ruth was a busy woman. Like most days, today she was wearing a belted dress with tiny print, flats, and a pale blue sweater. Henry laughed when Ruth called this her uniform. Smiling, he was warmed once again by the realization that he had it pretty good. Yep, he had it made in the shade and didn't take that fact for granted. Putting their empty coffee mugs in the dishwasher, he began climbing the stairs to see if he could offer his sergeant major any assistance corralling their brood.

Chapter Two

POWERS AND RULERS OF DARKNESS

> *For we wrestle not against flesh and blood, but against principalities, against powers, against the rulers of the darkness of this world, against spiritual wickedness in high places.*
>
> Ephesians 6:12

Click, click, click, his boots met the pavement. Heavily, in no hurry, the stranger made his way slowly down the lane, passing house after unsuspecting house, drawing closer to the end of the street. Nearing the church, the stranger's eyes found his handler, Dade, tucked in the murky folds of the shadows cast by the church. Tentatively, the stranger approached his master and instantly felt the familiar, suffocating wretchedness he always felt when close to Dade.

Neither of them spoke. It wasn't necessary. Dade's mere presence was enough, his making an appearance here, now, said it all. *You are mine. You will obey.* Dade's message was received loud and clear. They both knew why he, the stranger, was in Danport. They both knew what he was to do. This was a well-worn script for the stranger. His role, a character he'd played in countless other little communities. He knew his bit by heart.

Without warning, like Aladdin's genie returning to his bottle, Dade whirled to the left, vanishing beyond the door, which then melted into the earth, leaving the stranger alone, standing in the dark crevice of the building with the odor of sulfur still hanging in the air.

Chapter Three

A VIRTUOUS WOMAN, WHO CAN FIND?

Who can find a virtuous woman? For her price is far above rubies.

Proverbs 31:10

The pleasant fragrance of coffee met Ruth as she entered her kitchen to start breakfast. She drew her sweater in closer, warming her shoulders as there was a chill in the air this morning. As usual, she'd risen early so she'd have plenty of time to get her sizable brood ready for school, but apparently not as early as Henry. He must have made that pot of coffee before he left for his morning run. He was always so thoughtful. "Let's get a move on, troop. I expect you downstairs in thirty minutes; hop to it!" she bellowed over her shoulder in the direction of the stairs as she cracked another egg and began to whip with her whisk. Just as she was pouring the whipped eggs into the hot skillet, Henry bounded through the side door, dripping perspiration and puffing like a locomotive.

Jogging in place he said, "Mornin,' hon," then grinned as he tried to bring her in tight next to his sweat drenched chest.

Ruth giggled and hesitantly patted his wet t-shirt. "You'd better go shower; breakfast will be ready before you know it."

Henry rolled his eyes while wagging his head left to right, "Oh, all right," and with that, trotted up the stairs to the shower.

As Ruth buttered toast, the kids began to stumble toward the breakfast table. She poured each of them orange juice and then reached for her Bible. "Okay, guys, where were we? Let's see...."

Excited, Laci shouted, "Epeesion!"

"That's right. Yes, here it is, Ephesians 6:11, put on the full armor of God, so that you can take your stand against the devil's schemes. For our struggle is not against flesh and blood...."

Chapter Four

CHOSEN

Before I formed thee in the belly I knew thee; and before thou camest forth out of the womb I sanctified thee, and I ordained thee a prophet unto the nations.

Jeremiah 1:5

Pastor Scott put his key into the office door of the church. Community Church was his first church to pastor. He and Heather had moved to Danport six weeks ago. When he and Heather first arrived, he'd been on fire, full of hope and dreams, ready to make his mark and save Danport from a fiery hell. He'd hit the ground running and had come on a little strong, right out of the gate. Since then, at Heather's gentle suggestion, he'd been trying to tamp it down a little bit. He smiled as he remembered her saying, "You don't want them to flinch every time they see you coming, afraid you are going to slice them into a million little pieces with the *Sword of the Spirit*. Give them a chance to warm up to you, honey. Earn their respect, then maybe they'll listen to you and actually hear what you're trying to say to them."

Heather was perfect for him. He'd never known anyone who was more passionate about the Lord than his young wife. He'd loved her the moment their eyes met across the room of Fellowship Hall back in his home church. She'd been visiting her aunt that weekend, and the two of them had come to the church social. From his first sighting of her until now, he'd known she was his destiny. They were meant to be a team.

Waddling up behind him now as he opened the door, Heather was heavy with their first child. Holding the door open for her, they walked together into their church. *Their church.* He still couldn't believe it. His life had really done a 180, no doubt about it. Thinking back, he remembered how messed up he'd been after his last deployment overseas. Coming home, with all he'd seen and done while over there, had left him with a fiery wound he could only try to bury. He'd stuffed it deep down inside where it began to fester. Returning to reality and packed full of nightmares, regret and anger had not been a combination that worked out well for him, and eventually, he'd found himself sleeping in an alley outside an old warehouse, shooting up whatever he could find in an effort to numb the pain and dull the memories.

That's where James, a street preacher, found him. James was covered in military tattoos and wore a beard and a thick gray ponytail. At first, he'd just nudged Scott with the toe of his boot to see if he was still breathing. Scott remembered the dog with James, sniffing his chest and then licking his ears. Once James and his retired military dog, a Belgian Malinois named Sgt. Nubbs, found evidence of life, he'd invited Scott to dinner. After feeding Scott, James had shown him to the basement where the showers were located. Scott had never enjoyed anything more than the shower that day. The hot water and luxurious soap felt heavenly to him. When he dried off and walked out of the shower, he found deodorant, a toothbrush, toothpaste, and fresh clothing sitting in a chair, waiting for him in front of the bathroom door. Next to the chair, at full attention, was Sgt. Nubbs. Grateful for the fresh clothes, Scott dressed and then climbed the stairs back up to the soup kitchen where he'd eaten dinner earlier with James.

Cook handed him a note that read, *I'll be preaching tonight around seven o'clock at 612 Copenhagen. Sgt. Nubbs will show you the way. Drop by if you're interested. James.*

Scott *had* been interested and allowed Sgt. Nubbs to lead him straight away to the building on Copenhagen where his new friend was preaching. Walking in, he noticed the room was barely occupied, but James was already standing behind a lectern at the front of the room with his Bible open, biting at the bit to get started. That night James introduced himself and Sgt. Nubbs. Apparently, they'd served together in the Marines. James had been Sgt. Nubbs' handler.

After introductions, James preached as if he was in a grand arena full of people. James had been on fire. Billy Graham himself could not have done a better job or been more powerful. As he spoke, something began to tug at Scott's heart, and before he knew what was happening, tears were streaming down his cheeks.

Weeping, he accepted Christ that night, and there and then began the long struggle to pull his life together. Eventually, with a lot of help, he managed to get himself clean and employed. James mentored him in scripture, and Scott began to feel God's call, but to what? He wasn't exactly sure at the time. All he knew was that he wanted to be obedient to whatever the Lord's assignment might be. *Now, two years later, here I am, Pastor of Community Church, God help me*, Scott thought.

Heather set up his office at their new church within a week of their arrival and since then had been serving as his office manager, answering the phone, and printing bulletins. He really needed a secretary, but the Finance Committee had yet to find enough money in the church budget to swing a salary significant enough to tempt anyone to hire on. Lately, Heather's ankles only lasted through the morning. By afternoon they were so swollen, he'd been sending her home so she could prop up her feet.

The baby would be here in a couple of months, then he was not sure how he'd manage. "Here are the changes for the bulletin. Could you type it up for me and print them off Heather? By-the-way, I sure appreciate you, sweetheart. I'm not sure what I'll do down here without your help after the baby comes."

"You'll print them off yourself; you'll be just fine. You'll *be* fine," she said smiling.

Smiling back at her, his heart filled with warmth as he looked into her rounded and now, very full moon face. Walking back into his office, he heard Heather answer the phone, "Good morning. Community Church, how may I help you?" She had the sweetest spirit.

Knock, knock, knock. Opening his office door, Scott met the grinning, freckled, roseate face of Henry Pierce, Danport's handyman. "Good morning, Pastor. I'm here to fix that oven," Henry piped, reaching out to shake his pastor's hand.

"'Morning, Henry. I'll walk with you to the kitchen."

Picking up his toolbox, Henry and the pastor began to walk together down to the church's kitchen. "How's Heather fairing, Pastor?"

"Doing pretty well. She's had a little swelling in her ankles lately and so goes home in the afternoons to put up her feet."

Henry nodded knowingly, an expert by now on the maladies of pregnancy and childbirth. "How long's the oven been on the blink?"

"Sunday at the church breakfast seems to be when it all started. The biscuits never got done."

"Ahh...sounds like it may be the heating element then; I'll check it out. Say, do you have a minute?"

"Sure, Henry, what's up?"

Henry then shared with Pastor Scott about Ruth's experience yesterday with the stranger in the church sanctuary. Concerned, the pastor patted Henry on the shoulder and vowed to keep an eye out.

Chapter Five

WHITEWASHED SEPULCHRES

Woe unto you, scribes and Pharisees, hypocrites! For ye are like unto whited sepulchers, which indeed appear beautiful outward, but are within full of dead men's bones, and of all uncleanness. Even so ye also outwardly appear righteous unto men, but within ye are full of hypocrisy and iniquity.

Matthew 23:27-28

Buttoned up tightly in his tie, extra starched dress shirt and impeccably creased slacks, every hair of Richard's short *Ken-doll* haircut was in place, his chiseled face was freshly shaved, and his scent was Dark Lord by Kilian. He'd long ago decided he was worth the expense of fine cologne. Richard was a modern-day Pharisee. It was true that he did do a great deal of good, but he also wanted everyone to know about the great deal of good he did.

    He used his master key to enter the church and headed for the Prayer Room. It was critical that people in his position of leadership at the church have constant access to every part of the church facility, Richard thought smugly; thus, his insistence on having a key, a master key, no less. There was no place in this building he could not access. Nothing was off limits to him. He was in the building at all hours of the day and night, after all. This morning was his appointment in the Prayer Room. He was always prompt for his hour of prayer. Never missed it and made sure his arrival each week was duly noted. "Good morning, Heather," he sang too loudly as he passed the church office.

"'Morning, Brother Richard," Heather waved back with a warm smile.

Assessing her critically, Richard returned her wave, wiggling his fingers, but thought to himself, *she's as big as a barn*. He couldn't wait to tell his gorgeous little wife about the cow who was now answering the phone at their church. He could imagine them laughing together about how huge she was and so horribly plain, bless her heart. When his little Debbie had been pregnant with his child, she'd only gained seventeen pounds. He knew because he'd kept close tabs on her weight gain throughout all three of her trimesters. She'd done exactly as he'd instructed, like she always did, and with his wise guidance she'd managed to leave the hospital holding their new baby and wearing her pre-pregnancy dress slacks. He began to whistle down the hall of his church as he walked toward the Prayer Room. Upon entering, he was sure to sign his name with large, bold letters on the registry. Determined to focus his mind and heart, he began his hour of intercession by praising God. "Oh, God, You are so wise and have given me great responsibility...." Inevitably, his mind wandered to all of that great responsibility, and he was soon thinking about his many committees and duties at the church, projects he needed to get done and the timeline, when he had to have each of them wrapped up. Finally, completely distracted, he surrendered and went ahead and sat down at the desk in the small room and began making notes, lists of things that could simply not be ignored or forgotten. Before he knew it, his thoughts were absorbed with his pen and notepad, and he was writing furiously. Soon, there was a knock on the door and just like that, his hour was up. Dog-gone-it! Where had the time gone? The next prayer warrior was already at the door of the Prayer Room, ready to come in.

He turned the knob and opened the door to see Sister Jewell and cringed. "Good morning, Sister Jewell," he winced, holding his breath. *Sister Jewell never arrives anywhere without that dusting powder fragrance all over her. Do all old women wear that stuff,* he wondered?

"Rich-ard," she nodded curtly toward him as she wobbled by with a smirk on her face, headed toward the registry, her cane tapping in a nice little rhythm, falling in between each of her steps. Her miniature poodle, Snooky, was close behind her, his tiny toenails ticking along in perfect sixteenth note tempo to his mistress's pace. Arriving at the Prayer Room Registry, she scribbled her initials. Annoyed, Richard screamed in his head, *why does she always say my name that way? It's Richard. Richard. A single word, no break. Richard, and what on earth is that mangy mongrel of hers doing in the Prayer Room*? With that he hurriedly closed the door behind him, walked out of the church and to his car. He told himself that he would return to the church later to begin working on his *to do* list. Right now, however, he needed to make some hospital visits. A couple of church members had been admitted this week, and he wanted to make sure they knew he'd been praying for them, even though he'd never actually gotten around to *the praying for them* part. He'd been thinking about them, and besides, he *would* pray for them later, as soon as he could get everything done and clear his head.

Chapter Six

WHEN THOU PRAYEST

But thou, when thou prayest, enter into thy closet, and when thou hast shut thy door, pray to thy Father which is in secret; and thy Father which seeth in secret shall reward thee openly. But when ye pray, use not vain repetitions, as the heathen do: for they think that they shall be heard for their much speaking.

Matthew 6:6-7

Although she was elderly, Sister Jewell was still pretty sharp and was renowned for her wit and snappy responses. She and her husband, Charlie, a godly man, had been married for over 60 years. She missed him every day but was at peace knowing that she would join him one day soon. They'd raised three children together, children they were proud of. All three were self-supporting and loved God; that's about as much as a person could hope for, she supposed. Those years raising a family had been some of the best in Sister Jewell's estimation. She and Charlie had had a wonderful time during all of it, but as so often happens, Charlie passed away, all of their kids moved off, and she found herself old and alone. Although the kids did call often and try to come out to see her at least once a year, most of the time it was just she and Snooky, and so she occupied her days as best she could with ministry to her church family and neighbors. Snooky seemed to enjoy it as well, she thought, smiling. Snooky wasn't just a support animal--he was a *ministry pet*. That notion put a broad grin on her face as she mischievously thought about how much her little Snooky annoyed Richard. She winked at Snooky and ruffled his fur. "Good boy, Snooky, good boy," she chuckled.

Steadying herself, holding onto the desk in the Prayer Room, she knelt before a Throne that only she could see. In an unseen world that few even know exists, demons shrieked as they watched this mighty prayer warrior slowly humble herself and speak the Name. Once on her knees, she asked Holy Spirit to help her pray, and then with authority, she began to exalt the names of God. One after another they rolled off her tongue with ease. "I bless Your Name, Jehovah-Nissi, the banner over me. My mind is at peace because it is stayed on you, my Jehovah Shalom. I trust you, Father, because You are my Jehovah-Jireh. You are my provision manifest, You meet all my needs. I seek You, Jehovah-M'kaddesh, the One who sanctifies me and sets me apart for Your glory. For Your purpose alone, use me, God of the universe, King Jesus, my Alpha, and Omega...." It wasn't long before Sister Jewell was pleading the Blood and interceding for her pastor, her church, and its congregation. As she did so, a hedge of protection clapped into place, like a row of dominoes falling one after another. As if in a scene from a transformer movie, hinges creaked, walls slammed all around her position, constructing a wall of fire, connecting in concert like an umbrella over the church building, encasing the property, as well as those who worshipped there, with a bubble-like defense. Angels were dispatched to minister to brothers and sisters who were hurting or in need, and missionaries in far-away countries found doors that had once been closed to them, opening. Sister Jewell then went on to pray for the lost. "God, scripture says that no one comes to You unless You first draw them. Lord, please draw little Laci Pierce unto Yourself, place laborers in her path, transfer her from the Kingdom of Darkness into the Kingdom of your dear Son, Jesus," and so it went for the full hour as she named off one person after another, bringing their needs, temporal and eternal, before her Father.

Outside the Prayer Room's window, well beyond the spiritual hedge Sister Jewell had just prayed into place, an enraged demonic figure raked his face with bloody claws. Incensed, he beat his chest, howling in fury.

Chapter Seven
FIRST THINGS FIRST

But seek ye first the kingdom of God, and His righteousness; and all these things shall be added unto you.

Matthew 6:33

His mind racing, he felt the weight of having a wife and six kids to support. He tried not to be anxious, tried to cast all of his cares on the Lord, just like the Pastor explained Sunday; but it seemed like he inevitably took it all back each time, and then he'd begin fretting all the more. How would he ever pay this month's electric bill? Flipping on the oven in the church's kitchen, Henry bent down to see if he'd managed to fix it. Yep, it seemed to be working just fine. *Great, I have so many other customers to see this morning, I'm glad this job didn't take too long,* he thought as he picked up his tools and stored them in his toolbox. Walking by the Prayer Room, he noticed Sister Jewell just leaving. "Good morning, Sister Jewell; how are you feeling this fine day?"

"Doing well, young man. How are you managing with that large tribe of yours?"

"Trying my best, ma'am," Henry responded wistfully.

"That's a good laddie; you stay after it now, you hear? It is gonna work out just fine," she said knowingly with her crackly voice as she patted him gently on the shoulder. It was as if she had some sort of insider information, he thought, as he looked into her watery eyes before watching her totter quietly out the door, with Snooky trailing closely behind.

"Yes, ma'am, I sure will," Henry answered compliantly, noticing the Prayer Room was now empty. *I really should be on my way, I've got so many jobs to see about today, and we really need the money.* Even so, he felt drawn and so entered the room, closing the door behind him. Henry felt as though he'd walked into another dimension. A different matrix. What was that? It's candescent. A haze? But not one he could actually see. A fragrance? But with no scent. Music? With no sound. A presence? Yes, that's it. Before he knew it, he was bowing humbly, pouring out all of his worries and concerns, bringing all of his cares and petitions before God. He had no sense of time--it flew by. When he finally rose, he was bathed in a balm of calm and was able to leave all his anxiety there. Time seemed to stand still while he prayed. He noticed he was not late for his next stop. He wouldn't miss his next appointment. Feeling refreshed, Henry exited the room, thanking God, and went on to his following job at Sheriff McGowan's. He'd been told that the refrigerator at the police station was acting finicky, and Henry was now up to the task.

Chapter Eight

MISSION STATEMENT: KILL, STEAL, AND DESTROY

The thief cometh not, but for to steal, and to kill, and to destroy: I am come that they might have life, and that they might have it more abundantly.

John 10:10

A cup of steaming coffee was on the table in front of the stranger who sat in the back booth of Sally's Café. While there, he noticed the man from last night, the one he'd seen praying with that church lady and her family at their dinner table. This morning, he was in coveralls, walking briskly by the café's front window, carrying a toolbox, content with his mission. He was on task.

Taking a sip of his hot coffee, the stranger mournfully pondered his life. How had he gotten to this point? He considered the good people of this town, Dade's strategic plans for them, his own involvement and personal future. It was at this point that despondency swallowed him. Like always, Dade had been clear. There was no doubt in the stranger's mind about why he was in Danport or his assignment: havoc, devastation, and ruin. Kill, steal, and destroy. He had no choice. There was no other path for him, no turning back. He was bound.

Holding a full pot of coffee, ready to pour more into his cup, the pretty waitress with the sad eyes, interrupted his thoughts, "Warmer, mister?" Her name tag read Sally. *Sally. Of course. This must be her place*, he thought.

Waving her away, "No." Getting up, he threw a couple of bills on the table and made his way out the front door of her little café.

Holding the pot of coffee, Sally watched the stranger leave. One of her frequent customers, Matthew, brushed passed the stranger as he walked out the door of her café. Sidling up beside Sally, Matthew followed her gaze and thought to himself that you really never knew about people or what they were dealing with. Off handedly, he said to her, "I wonder what's his story."

Full of her own secrets, Sally shook her head and said, "Let me clean that table off for you, Matthew. The usual?"

Chapter Nine
TALEBEARER

The words of a talebearer are as wounds, and they go down into the innermost parts of the belly.

Proverbs 18:8

Buzzzz, buzzzz, zzzz. A swarm of anarchy buzzed about in the unseen world surrounding her. A barge of a woman, the spinster seemed to nurture confusion. Often wearing a little round netted hat, a skirt and a short blazer, her attire seemed to only accentuate her gargantuan hind quarters. Her massive size did not hinder her speed or agility in the least as she whipped from one controversy and onto another. This morning, she was on a mission. Her pumps were pounding down the hall as she stormed toward the church office when Pastor Scott saw her. He recognized her rigid posture, the tension in her neck, the pulsing veins, the prune-like pursing of her lips and was instantly on edge. Joselyn Boland had landed in their midst in full assault mode, and his defenses were immediately up. "Pastor, Pastor," she screeched, her disparaging eyes searching wildly until falling on Heather, who was busy jotting down a message as she balanced the phone between her jaw and upraised shoulder. Brimming with self-importance, Sister Joselyn burst into the office and shrieked, "Where is Pastor Scott, Heather, I simply must talk to him now," to which Heather lifted her hand, palm facing Joselyn, pencil between her fingers, in an effort to bring some semblance of quiet so she could finish with her phone conversation. "Well, I never," Sister Joselyn spouted, her cheeks puffy and flushed as she whipped around, scouting for Pastor Scott.

It was time for him to intervene. Bracing himself, the gentle man of God whispered a quick prayer, and with his hand extended toward her, came out of hiding and approached Sister Joselyn, "Good morning, Sister Joselyn, did you need to speak with me?"

The horse was out of the gate. That was all the invitation Sister Joselyn needed. She immediately launched into what had spurred today's tactical strike. "Someone has changed my floral arrangement at the front of...."

At just this moment, Heather caught his eye and with a quick glance, conveyed that she was struggling to hear the person talking to her on the phone, what with all of Sister Joselyn's yawping right in front of her desk. "Sister Joselyn," Pastor Scott said softly, placing his hand on her elbow, and guiding her into his inner office, "perhaps we could continue this discussion in my office."

"Harrumph, ahem, uh well, yes, of course," she stammered as she bolted about-face and pointed herself toward the pastor's office. No sooner did he get settled behind his desk, than Sister Joselyn's bombardment began. It was soon obvious that she had rehearsed her talking points for today's blitz as she began to knock them out one by one as if rattling through an outline--bang, pow, biff. She clattered off all the frailties and countless weaknesses of various church members of which she'd become aware, "...and I felt duty bound Pastor Scott to let you know straight away that Brother Fredrick was seen Saturday evening with Margaret Becker, who was wearing a highly inappropriate...."

On and on it went until, Pastor Scott, hoping for a reprieve, lifted both hands in surrender, gesturing for her to cease and desist. "Sister Joselyn, Sister Joselyn, dear me, we don't want to risk maligning our brothers and sisters. We can't be sure about these things you've mentioned, and even if we were sure, scripture reminds us that love covers. But let's not assume anything, and strive to think the best of others, shall we? I'm sure I can trust you to share these concerns of yours with no one else but God. Why don't we pause right now and pray together for these brothers and sisters who have burdened your heart so deeply," and with that Pastor Scott began to bow his head.

Sputtering to a sudden halt, completely shut down, Sister Joselyn smashed her lips together tightly, her cheeks bloated like balloons, her face reddened into a bright ruby and her eyes were bulging to the point that her pastor feared she might stroke. She had not expected to meet her match today. It seemed this new Pastor was not going to be as receptive as the ones before him, who had seemed to value her input. She was outraged and instantly felt an all-consuming dislike for him. Despite her sudden loathing for the man, somehow, she managed to squeak out through gritted teeth, "Well, of course, Pastor. You can certainly count on me," and bowed her head in prayer. After the amens, she stiffly excused herself, and with unexpected grace, managed to amble her enormous mass through the door, nodding a "Good day," to Heather as she exited out of the church office.

Chapter Ten
SPIRITS OF DEVILS

For they are the spirits of devils, working miracles, which go forth unto the kings of the earth and of the whole world, to gather them to the battle of that great day of God Almighty.
Revelation 16:14

It was dark as Sheriff McGowan walked slowly back down the main street of Danport, anxious to get home to Harriett and Liam. This was his last round of the day before going home for supper. Harriett had promised him some of her famous freezer stew, which he'd looked forward to all day. His stomach growled ferociously in anticipation. It amazed him that something so simple could be so absolutely delicious. Harriett collected their leftover vegetables from each meal for a couple of weeks in a big Tupperware she kept in the freezer. A cup of green beans one evening, half a cup of corn the next and before they knew it, they had a hodgepodge tub full and were ready to make stew. When the mixture was finally to the top of the Tupperware bowl, she dumped it all into their crockpot, added whatever else hit her fancy, and voila! It was outstanding! She usually let it simmer throughout the day and by the evening, it was ready for supper and proved to be some of the best eating this side of the Mississippi River. A bowl of Harriett's freezer stew placed along-side a cast iron skillet of her homemade scratch cornbread, and you had yourself a man's kind of meal. She'd known from the start that the way to his heart was via his stomach.

Checking locks as he continued his last round, he looked for anything out of place as he walked down the sidewalk of Danport. Sauntering down his nightly path, Sheriff McGowan thought back to the days when he and Harriett were young and just getting started. They'd been sweethearts all through college, even though he'd gotten a late start because he didn't begin until after serving in the Air Force. Though she was younger than he, Harriett was very mature, beautiful and wise beyond her years. He and Harriet were quickly an item.

They'd both pursued degrees in Criminal Justice. Her interest had leaned more toward the juvenile delinquency end, and he'd been more interested in criminal investigation, but they'd found themselves in several of the same classes while going through school. He tried and tried to get the courage to ask her out until she finally got tired of waiting and invited him over for dinner. The moment he walked into her apartment and smelled the aroma of delicious foods cooking, he'd knew this was the gal for him. They spent that evening talking about any and everything until it was way beyond a suitable hour. Conversation had always been so easy with Harriett that time often just seemed to fly by. That was the beginning of some of the best years of Jack's life. He'd fallen head over heels in love with the cute little crime busting redhead.

When they got the job offer to run the sheriff's department in the small community of Danport, it had seemed like a dream come true, and Harriett's knowing her way around a squad car and how to handle a Glock had proven an added benefit over the years. He often had her by his side, serving as his deputy. She didn't seem to mind riding shotgun and helping him out. Besides, Danport was generally pretty quiet. The few times there had been a crisis in Danport, Harriett had been unflappable. In fact, between the two of them, she was probably the better law officer. Her grades had certainly been better than his all through college.

As he jiggled the drugstore's doorknob to make sure it was locked, he thought about the day they both graduated; it seemed like it was only yesterday. She'd finished summa cum laude, and he couldn't have been more proud. There they'd both stood, dressed in their caps and gowns, surrounded by family and friends who were busy congratulating them, when Jack suddenly dropped to one knee, took her free hand in his and popped the question, "Will you marry me, Harriett?"

With her diploma in one hand and her free hand in Jack's, Harriett nodded her affirmation and managed to croak out a "Yes," which was followed by a giant "Hoorah," surely heard throughout the campus as the crowd of family and friends gathered around them erupted, filling the air with happy sounds of good wishes and approval.

Their wedding had been small with just a few close relatives and classmates convening in a little country church just outside of Riverside. He'd asked a campus pastor he knew to do the wedding, Charlie Winslow. Charlie was older and had been a part of campus ministry the whole time Harriett and Jack attended school. He was often seen handing out Bibles or just sitting in the student union visiting or praying with students. All the kids really liked Charlie; he was the real deal.

The wedding was so small that Jack and Harriett decided to do it all themselves, so they picked up the key to the venue, did all the decorating, fixed the punch, and bought the cake at a local bakery for their tiny reception afterwards. Harriett had wanted to bake the cake herself, too, and Jack had no doubt she would've created a masterpiece, but he'd convinced her to buy the cake instead so she wouldn't be completely worn out by the time she walked down the aisle.

The day of the wedding arrived, and there were Charlie and Jewell Winslow bright and early, waiting at the front of the church when Jack arrived to unlock the door. "Good morning, son. Are you ready for your big day?"

"I suppose," Jack smiled nervously.

"Now, now, none of that. Be bold. Do not fear or be dismayed. Let's do this," Charlie commanded. As soon as the church doors were opened, Charlie and Jewell got out their bottles of anointing oil and began praying over the sanctuary where the wedding was to take place, anointing each pew as they went down the center aisle.

Watching the older couple move through the sanctum, Jack thought, what a beautiful scene. Who would ever have thought? How generous of Charlie and Jewell to come early and take the time to do this! They were genuinely good people.

Jack's brother, Joel, stood up for him as his best man that day; they'd always been close. Jack had been especially thankful to have him nearby when the organ hit the first few chords of the Bridal Chorus because his knees involuntarily buckled. Fortunately, his brother grabbed his elbow, preventing his collapse as he whispered, "Easy, buddy," in support.

Jack had never seen a more beautiful bride, his bride, he couldn't believe it. She'd been radiant in her mother's wedding gown, and Jack had been spellbound, unable to take his eyes off the stunning woman who'd agreed to be his wife. Once the *I Do's* were delivered and, in the book, and the new bride and groom, Harriett and Jack, were toodling down the road with tin cans clanging behind their car, they relived the special service with which Charlie had blessed them. What a gift! It seemed like a worship service, a covenant. Charlie explained how marriage was a type-shadow of Christ's love for the church. It had been beautiful. Enchanting. He and Harriett would always treasure their memory of the ceremony, given to them by Charlie.

Their honeymoon had been in a simple cabin that belonged to a friend of Charlie's. They'd only had a few days together there in the Colorado mountains, but in Harriett's retelling, there had never been anything more romantic. They woke up each morning to a misty fog that hovered over the green carpet of grass just off their front porch with deer grazing nearby. The graceful animals would glance occasionally over at Harriett and Jack, completely unafraid. She and Jack sat together each morning, wrapped in a quilt on the porch swing, sharing a cup of coffee as they greeted the day. It had been magical.

They returned to a job offer from the city of Danport, where Charlie and Jewell lived. Jack had no doubt Charlie had helped him get this job by putting in a good word for him, and Jack had been running the Danport Sheriff's Department ever since. Jack had so many reasons to thank Charlie Winslow, his mentor and friend. He'd done so much for him.

Once he and Harriett were settled in Danport, Charlie invited Jack over to study scripture with him. They met once a week right up until the day Charlie died. Jack had been devastated by the loss of his friend, but despite his deep sorrow, honored and grateful when Sister Jewell asked him to give the eulogy at Charlie's funeral. Jack had so much he wanted to say. He only hoped God opened a portal in heaven that day and allowed Charlie to lean over the rail and listen to all he'd expressed during the service, because Jack poured out his heart describing Charlie, the man of God he'd come to respect and know so well. A huge crowd gathered to pay their respects and plenty of amens were expressed at the funeral as Jack spoke. Charlie touched so many lives.

Jack hit rock bottom and spiraled around the drain of life for quite a while after losing Charlie. Feeling sorry for himself, grieving the loss of his dear old friend, he'd moped around until one day Sister Jewell stopped by the Sheriff's office, where she found Jack still down in the dumps. Without hesitation, she whacked his calf with her cane, causing it to sting and welt up and told him to get a grip. With her frowning at him sternly in disapproval, he'd done just that. He began to realize right then and there that Charlie wouldn't want him to continue to mourn, but instead Charlie would want Jack to rejoice with him, *for* him, because Charlie was exactly where he'd wanted to be his whole life. After all, death has no sting for people like Charlie. Now, it was time for Jack to step up and carry the torch. Since then, it hadn't always been easy, but Jack had tried to walk in the footsteps of Charlie as best he could.

Continuing his stroll through Danport, looking into windows as the evening got later, he thought about his boy, Liam. Now thirty and a grown man, Liam would always be with Harriett and him. They'd known immediately from the very beginning that Liam was going to be a special blessing to them. Liam was born with Downs syndrome and a hearing deficiency.

As was so often the case in such instances, in the years since Liam's birth, Jack and Harriett had learned so much from him. The purity in which he viewed everything and his unconditional love for everyone had given Harriett and Jack a whole new perspective. Liam had opened their eyes.

Refocusing on the task at hand, Jack stepped up to the next business, checked the store front lock, making sure it was secure, and then shone his flashlight inside the window, looking for anything that might seem out of place. He'd been doing this for over 30 years and so could easily pick up on anything that wasn't quite right or out of order, something that rarely happened in Danport, the small community in his charge. This was his town, and he liked to make sure it was all buttoned down tightly before he called it a night.

Out of the corner of his eye he saw movement and swiftly turned his head to see two figures engrossed in conversation in the shadows of the church, although they didn't seem to actually be talking. Their lips weren't moving, and yet Sheriff McGowan was sure they were communicating. One of them looked like the stranger Henry had described to him earlier. He was with someone else now, but it was hard to discern who. Suddenly, the figure with the stranger was gone. Poof! The stranger stood alone, and for the first time seemed to become aware of the Sheriff's close proximity. "Everything all right over there, sir?"

"Yes, officer. All is well. Good evening," the stranger nodded his head to the sheriff and slipped passed him quickly.

As he felt the stranger sweep by, brushing the sleeve of his shirt, Sheriff McGowan reflexively shuddered as an uncomfortable shiver tingled down his spine. What was that about? Who was this guy to give him such a bad case of the creeps? Over the years, Sheriff McGowan had learned to pay attention to those sorts of gut reactions and decided he better check out the area.

Walking over to the place where the two, only moments ago had been standing near the church, his nostrils were immediately assaulted by a terrific pungent odor. Sulfur. He noticed that the grass was indented where their feet had been. Two sets. He pressed his fingers against the flat grass where the apparition had been standing and felt unusual heat. So, his eyes hadn't been playing tricks on him. He hadn't imagined another--what? Another man? Something had been standing here with the stranger. But where had that something gone? Whatever it was, it seemed to have just vanished into the seam of the church building right here somehow. He ran his flashlight up and down the area of the building that had opened up earlier like a door. Was that smoke seeping out of that line, that junction in the building? Sniffing that intersection, Sheriff McGowan's automatic reflex was to quickly draw back. Decomposition. Rot. Overcome with apprehension, he stepped away from the corner, staring at the line of cement that affixed the two walls of brick together. What was going on here? What was he experiencing? He felt an urgency to retreat. To run fast as far from this place as he could. Goodness, what was wrong with him? He was a grown man; he wasn't some kind of coward afraid of the boogie man. The thoughts he was having were ridiculous. Crazy stuff. Get a grip, man. Spirits? Supernatural? Demonic? What? He shook his head, laughing at himself.

Feeling silly he walked home for his evening hug from Liam and a bowl of Harriett's freezer stew, assuring himself that everything would look more wholesome in the morning. His confidence in that vow grew stronger with each step taken away from the church.

Chapter Eleven

THE SABBATH

Not forsaking the assembling of ourselves together, as the manner of some is; but exhorting one another: and so much the more, as ye see the day approaching.

Hebrews 10:25

The Pierce household was percolating in a well-rehearsed rhythm on this fine Sunday morning. It was obviously not the first time Henry's little clan had tried to be on time to church. They tried every single Sunday but rarely hit the mark. Mates to socks had to be hunted down, spots scrubbed off ties, hair wet, parted and combed, belts located under beds, and Adam was drinking out of the milk carton again. "Adam! I declare, how many times have I told you? Oh, Adam, you're spilling it all over your nice shirt; now you're gonna sour and stink. Laci, get your teeth brushed. Isabella, let me tie that for you, darling. Nope, nope, nope, Joey, not that shirt..." and so it went, every single Sunday morning.

Henry honestly didn't know how Ruth kept her sanity. He was about to lose his, just listening to all the commotion. Finally, they were all clean, brushed, straightened, tucked, and walking together toward Church. "Good morning, Pastor Scott," Ruth said as she shook her pastor's hand at the front door of the church before turning to hug his wife, Heather. "You're glowing this morning, Heather, how are you feeling? Are those ankles still swelling on ya?" Ruth guided Heather over to the side out of the ear shot of the men and passersby so they could confide in one another.

Finally, the congregation was all inside and seated. After Matthew led those gathered together in a few hymns, he winked at the young pianist, Alice, and they left the stage area and sat down together on the front row. Pastor Scott then stepped up to the podium. "Good morning, Church," he exclaimed, smiling broadly. "This is the day our Lord has made, let us rejoice and be glad in it. Henry, let's pass the offering plates." Soon the tithes and offerings had been collected and Henry, dress-shirt frayed around the collar, took the offering plates full of money to the back of the church for counting. It was at about this moment that Pastor Scott left the pulpit area, walked around it, and sat down on the stage's step directly in front of the pulpit. Loosening his tie and unbuttoning his top button, he said, "This morning I'd like you to open your Bibles to Ephesians 6."

Richard Langley was appalled. *What, what is Pastor doing? What does our pastor think we are, hippies? Or does he think we're at a bar? You'd think he'd try to wear a better fitting suit. A man of God really should look smart. Those Pierce children are driving me crazy. Look at that little brat, Adam, smiling. He's all sticky this morning, smells like sour milk, and, of course, wanted to hug me. Why can't Henry and Ruth control him?*

Sister Joselyn Boland mumbled under her breath, "Unbelievable," as she watched her pastor get comfortable on the stage's step and flip open the pages of his Bible to Ephesians, for what he termed *their study*.

Sally, looking different this morning as she was dressed in something other than her waitressing t-shirt and jeans, listened intently to Pastor Scott, hoping against hope to find a way out of the dark hole she now found herself in. A black cloud seemed to follow her, hover over her. She couldn't recall being authentically happy even once since her mother had been diagnosed. She'd forgotten how it felt to be content, to know joy. It would be wonderful. Freeing.

Brother Fredrick and Margaret Becker sat together on the right side of the church, fourth pew back, shoulder to shoulder, looking straight ahead. Margaret's little boy sat beside her this morning. Ben was sitting quietly, coloring with the crayons Fred had brought for him; he was such a good man. She had been pleased by the attention Fred had been showing little Ben, taking him fishing and working with him to build a fort. Ben really needed a father figure in his life, and Fred seemed to be enjoying that role.

Margaret had observed Fred putting money into the offering plates each Sunday morning and so this morning, felt good about following his example and added what little bit she could manage into the gold platter as it was passed by her. She thought to herself how much she'd been enjoying the Bible study she and Fred had been having together each week and the small group they'd been attending at the Pierce's. She'd never known a man like Fred.

Sister Joselyn glared at the back of Brother Fredrick and Margaret's heads. She could not believe her eyes when the two of them walked into the church together again all hoity toity and with her little boy again, like it was perfectly all right. *Didn't Margaret's mother teach her anything about right and wrong? What a tramp! She is surely leading Brother Fredrick down the wrong path.* Buzz, buzz, buzz.

Lauren hung her head in deep despair and sighed. No one knew. It was her terrible, terrible secret. Here in the sanctuary, she was surrounded by people all of whom seemed to have happy little lives while she was living in an inescapable nightmare. She felt as if she might scream out the horror she faced regularly but then noticed blood seeping through her sleeve. Oh, no! She smashed against it hard, applying pressure. After he'd left her last night, she'd gone into the bathroom to cut. She'd had to. Needed to. The release she'd felt last night with that first slash to her arm had been immediate. She pressed harder against the self-inflicted wound, applying more force. *Not here, stop bleeding, please stop!*

The stranger sat alone in the back pew thinking, calculating. He had been observing and had begun to develop his plan of action. He'd located the church's weak links but also knew from experience that sometimes the soft spots were not what one might expect. The real trophy, sometimes, was the more virtuous saint. Get one of them to stumble, and the impact on the body was astounding. The givers, merciful and servant types could be used very effectively at times if orchestrated just right. It was funny in a sick sort of way; he usually found the same characters in each fellowship assigned to him. Wherever his sovereign stationed him, he always found the proud ones and the bitter gossips, the legalistic Pharisee, or the guy who was living from paycheck to paycheck, the easily manipulated, the vulnerable, the desperate, the evil, and the righteous. They were in every church. There was also always a remnant, that genuine believer or two, the Prayer Warriors. He tried to steer clear of them. They were way too discerning. He'd been making mental notes, collecting intel he'd use to accomplish his mission here. Dade had been right; Danport was ripe for the pickin'. Why did people have to be so easy to take advantage of, so easy to influence and manipulate? The stranger hung his head in morose anguish as Pastor Scott continued to read and teach from Ephesians.

"In closing, Church, I'd like to encourage each of you to meet with your small group this week. I've prepared an outline on Ephesians for your discussion time. Maybe it'll help those of you who are facilitating the discussions. You can pick those sheets up at the back of the church as you leave today." With that, Pastor Scott stood and stretched out his hand, palm toward his congregation, and prayed, "Now, may the Lord bless and keep you, make His face to shine upon you, be gracious to you, and give you peace...."

Ruth found the stranger's eyes from across the sanctuary, and for a moment the two of them were locked in a gaze that spoke volumes. In mere moments she sensed the depth of his desperation. His years of suffering cascaded like falling tiles, one after another banging down to her very core. She shuttered involuntarily, and he looked away. After the pastor concluded the benediction, the stranger began to leave the building.

Without warning the stranger smelled the putrid odor that could mean only one thing. Reeling around, he saw Dade by the stained-glass windows, laughing at him. The delight Dade seemed to derive from his torment was evident and unyielding. Startled by a tap on his shoulder the stranger turned around. Henry and Ruth, obviously unable to see Dade, met him with extended hands and smiles, introducing themselves and inviting him to join their small group meeting on Wednesday evening at 6:00. "Thank you, yes, I'd like that. I'll see you then," the stranger managed to spit out before quickly excusing himself and fleeing through the crowd of exiting congregants.

"Funny," Ruth said to Henry, "he didn't even ask where we live or tell us his name."

About that time Sister Jewell walked up to the couple holding their little Isabella's hand and laughing. "This tiny bean just about escaped," she grinned, directing Isabella to go to her mother. Her eyes clouded with concern as she followed Ruth's stare after the stranger. "I'm gonna be praying for you, dearie. You take care now."

Brother Fredrick, Margaret, and young Ben stepped up in line to shake Pastor Scott's hand. Fredrick proudly bragged on Ben to the Pastor, "He's seven, Pastor, and can already bait his own hook and cast it. You wouldn't believe the catfish he caught yesterday."

Pastor Scott said, "That's awesome, Ben! Maybe I can join you two sometime down on the creek and you can give me a few pointers, young man."

"Wouldn't that be nice, Ben?" Margret asked.

Ben nodded his head shyly.

Pastor asked, "How 'bout next weekend?"

"It's a date, then," said Brother Fredrick.

Sister Joselyn and Richard eyed each other in disbelief. "You've got to be kidding me," Sister Joselyn complained under her breath before loudly pushing up to the pastor. "Hello, Pastor, excellent sermon. I'd say you hit it right out of the ballpark this morning." *Especially when you left the pulpit and sat on the floor. Oh, my goodness. Start going barefoot next and it's over, I'll be outta here.*

Sally tried to smile as she stepped up next in line and shook Pastor Scott's hand at the door of the sanctuary before walking down the front steps of the church to go to her home over the café. She didn't know if she'd ever felt more despondent and alone. The sermon was great, but she still felt like she was in a dark hole. Just as her foot hit the last step in front of the church before the sidewalk, a little old lady patted her elbow. "Good morning, young lady. I'd like to introduce myself; most people call me Sister Jewell, and you are?"

"Um, hello, I'm Sally ma'am, how do you do?"

"I do just fine and would be pleased to have you join me for lunch today, if you're free?"

"Well, I don't know, I, uh, well, yes, yes, of course, that would be lovely," Sally said, and the two of them walked off together. Sister Jewell looped her arm in the crook of Sally's as her cane tapped time to their easy going pace.

Upon entering Sister Jewell's small home, just a block from the church, Sally's mouth began to water as she smelled the simmering crockpot full of corn chowder. Sister Jewell instructed her to sit at the very clean round table in her kitchen where a place had already been set for her as if she'd been expected. Iced tea with mint was next placed by her knife and spoon, and soon crackers, cheese and raw vegetables were added to the table's spread. As Sister Jewell ladled chowder into bowls, she hummed softly to herself, completely at ease and in absolutely no hurry. Positioning a beautiful bowl of steaming yellow chowder in front of Sally, Sister Jewell maneuvered into her own chair while saying, "Tell me about yourself, young lady."

Chapter Twelve

EMBRACE THE CHAOS

Thou wilt keep him in perfect peace, whose mind is stayed on thee: because he trusteth in thee.

Isaiah 26:3

It was pandemonium at the Pierce's home, but then, when was it not? Every day was wild and crazy. Sunday afternoons, however, were generally chaos to the tenth power. Mayhem and then some. A regular day on a double shot of espresso. The Pierce household was in an uproar. Ruth used to try for a genuine sabbath on the sabbath, but long ago surrendered to the Sunday tsunami that seemed to be symptomatic of her large, active family. As she listened to the search and seizure of baseball bats and cleats underway overhead, she began slapping sandwiches together. That was about all they'd have time for today before heading out to the baseball diamond for Adam and Joey's game. Peanut butter and jelly, ham and cheese, turkey and cheese, cheese only, and what was it Laci liked? Oh, yes, bologna with extra mustard. She called it a bologna soufflé. Ruth laughed to herself about that. Obviously, Laci didn't have a clue what a soufflé really was. As

Ruth continued preparing lunch, she gave thanks once again for Sister Jewell's delivery yesterday of lunch meats and slices of cheese. How had she known? It was just what they'd needed to make it to the end of this month. What a blessing that sweet lady was.

Oh, my goodness, what had become of the time! "Let's go, team; we'll have to eat on the way," she barked, and within moments they were each one heading out the door, sandwich in hand, running toward the family's minivan.

Chapter Thirteen

HUSBANDS, LOVE YOUR WIVES

Husbands, love your wives, even as Christ also loved the church, and gave himself for it.

Ephesians 5:25

Pastor Scott tucked an extra squashy pillow behind the small of Heather's back, then sat down on the other end of their couch, laying Heather's feet in his lap. Kneading the arches of the bottom of her feet he said, "How does toast and scrambled eggs sound? I think I can manage that. You sit right here and stay off these feet."

"I adore scrambled eggs. You don't have to tell me twice. I'll stay right here for the duration of the afternoon. Thank you, sweetheart," Heather purred, closing her eyes.

Scott rose from the couch, covered her feet with a throw blanket and walked into their kitchen.

Heather felt so frustrated. She'd gained more weight than she'd wanted to gain. The reflection that met her in the mirror each morning was a moon faced, exaggerated version of her former self. Her lips looked like they belonged on a Pufferfish. Honestly, she felt like an enlarged marshmallow. Ugh! The doctor didn't seem too concerned, but it was awfully hard watching her body swell up like a toad. Interrupting her thoughts, the baby moved a tiny elbow across the width of her rounded, very distended belly. She watched in awe as the mound could be seen racing from one side to the other. Maybe the baby was rolling over? Amazing! "Oh, honey, hurry, come see!"

Clad in a cute little frilly apron and holding a whisk, Scott appeared in the kitchen door. "What is it?"

Pointing at her belly, Heather said, "Look. She's moving."

Smiling, he rushed to her side saying, "She?"

Heather giggled, "Maybe, I guess we'll see. Come, put your hand right here."

Laying his palm in the baby's most recent path, he felt the baby move beneath his hand, his eyes widened, and he was filled with the wonder fathers often experience when first feeling the movement of their child. What a blessing! Part him. Part Heather. It was a miracle. The dawning of a sober revelation awakened in him. "She's us. Part you, part me. A sacred trust with which God has gifted us to mold and shape. What a gigantic responsibility." He shook his head and looked down. "I don't know, I just don't know if I'm up to it."

"You'll do fine. I've no doubt you'll be an incredible father. Now march right back into the kitchen and scramble us up some eggs."

"Yes, ma'am," he saluted.

Chapter Fourteen

EL ROI: GOD WHO SEES ME

Thine eyes did see my substance, yet being unperfect; And in thy book all my members were written, which in continuance were fashioned, when as yet there was none of them.

Psalm 139:16

Finishing off the last of Margaret's tuna casserole, young Ben asked to be excused from the table. "Of course, Ben, that would be fine; please carry your plate into the kitchen for me. Thank you, shug."

Ben obediently walked into the kitchen with his dinner plate. "He's such a good boy, Margaret. You've done an excellent job raising him. I know it hasn't been easy," Fredrick added.

"Thank you. No, it hasn't. In fact, it's been a real challenge. When I found out I was pregnant, I wasn't sure how we'd make it, but somehow, we've managed."

"What's your story, Margaret? Or perhaps you don't want to talk about it. Maybe I'm being too nosy?"

"You certainly are not. All this time and you've never asked about him. You've earned our trust, Fred. Besides, you feel safe. You have a right to know at this point," Margaret concluded. "I was young and stupid, I guess, is the best place to begin. I'd just started college when a friend invited me to a fraternity party. I accepted the invitation and when I got there, I felt like the belle of the ball. Guys seemed to be paying special attention to me, the music was loud, the dancing frantic, they were feeding me drinks. Apparently, at some point I blacked out. Woke up the next morning in an upstairs bedroom of the frat house in someone's bed. My blood ran cold when I realized my clothes were strewn all over the room. I had no idea what had happened, how many, or who they were, but I was sore, bruised and knew. I mean, there was little doubt in my mind that I'd been set up, drugged, and abused throughout the night."

"Did you report it to the police?"

"No. For some reason I felt embarrassed, so foolish and ashamed. Like it was my fault for being so naïve. Six weeks later I learned I was pregnant."

"Oh, dear. What did you do? Was there anyone to help you?"

"I had girlfriends I was able to confide in who helped me as best they could, supported me. Most of them advised I get an abortion, and I gotta admit, I thought about it."

Fredrick smiled. "Obviously, you didn't take their advice. Why not?"

Margaret sighed, "I couldn't. Look, I'll admit, I may not have always lived like I should, but I do believe in God, so my faith played a big part in my decision not to get an abortion. But to be honest at that time in my life, faith in God wouldn't have been enough to keep me from terminating and extinguishing all of my problems. You know what did it for me?"

"Tell me."

"I was still undecided but continuing to see my doctor when it came time for an ultrasound. During the exam, as she was rolling all over my belly, she said, 'Listen to this, Margaret. You've got to hear this.' When she put her headsets on me, I heard my baby boy, Ben, humming."

"Humming? You know I'm a doctor, right? I mean, there's a heartbeat pretty early, sure enough, but humming?" Fredrick laughed.

"Hey, don't rain on my parade. Ben was humming, OK?

Smiling, Fred put his hands up defensively, "Alright, Alright."

"Anyway, I knew right then and there, that I couldn't do it, 'cause the heart of an innocent little human being, my Ben, was beating inside of my belly and singing for crying out loud," Margaret said with a laugh. "A sense of maternal protectiveness overwhelmed me. Believe me, I was as surprised as anybody, but by that point, I knew I couldn't go through with an abortion, not me, but that's not an indictment of my friends who've chosen that route. I'm not an activist or whatever. It just wasn't the answer for me is all."

"What about your parents? Have they been around to help you?"

"They both died when I was very young. Car wreck. I was still a kid, but too old to be attractive to couples wanting to adopt, so I grew up in foster care," responded Margaret.

"Oh, wow! I'm so sorry. So, you really *are* a single mom. Alone. It really would've been more convenient, less awkward for you to abort," Fredrick said with compassion.

"In some ways maybe, but that was not the solution for me. I think it would've gotten to me eventually, ya know? Wounded my heart if that makes sense? I also looked into adoption during the first couple of months of my pregnancy, thought that might be my best option, but maybe because I grew up in foster care? I don't know why for sure, but I just had this yearning to raise my own child and the bigger I grew, and believe me I got pretty huge, the more he moved inside me, the more in love with him I became. By the time he was born, I was certain I couldn't give him up. I couldn't live without him. My nightmare had become the best thing to ever happen to me. I quit school, moved to Danport, got the job at Dr. Mulligan's, and Ben and I've been doing life together ever since."

"I think you're very brave. Very courageous," Fredrick beamed. "Now, you sit right here and start reading that novel you've been wanting to get into. I'm gonna see if Ben would like to toss the baseball back and forth in the backyard for a little while."

Chapter Fifteen
PURE IN HEART

Blessed are the pure in heart: for they shall see God.
Matthew 5:8

Liam McGowan greatly admired his dad, the Sheriff of Danport. To him, his dad was as strong as any superhero, a mighty champion who always did the right thing. Whenever his dad expressed pride in him, Liam could feel it all the way down to his toes. There was nothing he wanted more than to bask in his dad's approval. He knew his dad had flown airplanes while in the service, so Liam had become intensely interested in putting model airplanes together. It had become his obsession because each time Liam finished a model airplane, his dad would just brag and brag on him as he held up his completed work for inspection. Sometimes, while holding Liam's airplane, his dad would launch into a story about the war or his time flying an aircraft while overseas in the Air Force. Liam lived for these moments.

Sitting now at his desk, Liam was concentrating very hard on the latest model airplane kit his dad helped him pick out. Liam could think of no better purchase he'd rather make than these model airplanes. He was the busboy at Sally's Café and was very good at saving his earnings. This was one of the things he regularly spent his money on. He now had several completed airplanes hanging by fishing wire from his bedroom ceiling. He'd been working on this latest model every free moment since getting it home. Sitting very still, the bright light on his desk shone on his work, helping him to see better as he examined it intently through the thick lens of his glasses.

Although Liam wore hearing aids, he still didn't hear well. Fortunately, his senses had adapted, and he heard or felt the rhythm of feet approaching his door before the knock. "Liam are you ready?" his mom asked.

"Ready, Freddy," piped Liam, grinning widely at his next favorite person in the world.

"Alright then, let's head that way. Who's Freddy, by-the-way?"

Laughing, Liam responded, "It's an expression, Puddin'tang," Liam always addressed his mother in this way.

"Have you finished your model airplane yet?"

"After while, Crocodile," Liam loved sayings, quotes, airplanes, and baseball.

Mrs. McGowan smiled and said, "Let's go, young man; we don't want to miss the first batter. You know how much Adam is counting on you to be at his game to cheer him on."

Addressing the airplane, he'd been gluing together, Liam said, "See you soon, Baboon."

As he and his mom drove to the baseball diamond, Liam quoted Yogi Berra, "Love is the most important thing in the world, but baseball is pretty good, too."

Smiling, Mrs. McGowan nodded in agreement and continued to drive down the street toward the baseball field where Liam's father, Jack, the Sherriff of Danport, was waiting.

Chapter Sixteen

TAKE ME OUT TO THE BALLPARK

"I see great things in baseball. It's our game, the American game."

-Walt Whitman

Crack! Adam smacked the ball out into left field and began running hard toward first base. He sped fast passed it and could hear his friend Liam hollering wildly as he ran as hard as he could toward the next base. Adam was soon sliding through the dirt, his cleats touching the mound on second just in time. Safe. Made it, a millisecond before the first baseman caught the incoming ball from right field and threw it hard to the second baseman. With one foot tapping the mound, he snuck a moment to look up and beamed at Liam in the stands with the Sheriff and Mrs. McGowan. Liam responded with a thumbs up.

Adam's brother, Joey, was up to bat next. "Come on, Joey, bring me home," hollered Adam to his younger sibling as he clapped his hands together. Joey chalked his grip, positioned himself over home base in batter up posture and concentrated, focusing on the pitcher winding up. Whoooshwit! The ball sizzled in the direction of home base. Joey sliced it perfectly, and it soared high toward the back fence in center field. It was an awesome sight, but Adam couldn't afford to admire Joey's fine work too long. With a huge grin on his face, he took off just as Joey turned with full force toward first base. Soon Joey was right behind Adam, as their feet pounded down the stretch, swoosh. First Adam, then Joey, both zooming across home base as the crowd went wild.

In the stands, Adam and Joey's mom, Ruth, wiped Sami's little fingers and gave Isabella her sippy cup. Henry began to help Laci reload her tiny backpack with the toys she'd asked to bring. One game down and on to the next event. It was time to pack up so they could all head to the soccer field for Jeannie's practice.

Just another typical Sunday afternoon for the Pierce family, Henry thought with a contented smile.

Chapter Seventeen
LOVE ONE ANOTHER

Finally, be ye all of one mind, having compassion one of another, love as brethren, be pitiful, be courteous.

1 Peter 3:8

After their Sunday luncheon, Sally left Sister Jewell's front porch and walked to her apartment above her café. She'd enjoyed the meal and her time with Sister Jewell today. She smiled, thinking to herself how nice it was to eat someone else's food for a change. She felt lighter, somehow. Better. Content. At peace. Sister Jewell's invitation to lunch had lifted her spirits. Love was not just a word, it was behavior, and Sister Jewell's compassion had helped Sally more than anything else so far. Sally nodded thinking to herself, *actions really do speak louder than words.*

Sister Jewell seemed to be a very wise old lady, no doubt about that, and she was so kind. She'd been genuinely interested in her, although she didn't probe, and she wasn't nosey. It was almost as if she already knew Sally's secret, but she couldn't possibly. Nevertheless, Sally kept her life and her past to herself. She sure wasn't ready to have *that* all over town, even though Sister Jewell didn't strike her as a gossip. Whatever, right now she didn't feel like reliving it all or sharing it with anyone, so light chit chat was best. She was thankful Sister Jewell hadn't pushed God on her or opened that can of worms, although she sensed Sister Jewell was very deep spiritually, and it made Sally curious to learn more, but not today. Nothing deep today. The conversation was easy surface stuff, yet even with that, Sally had to admit, she did feel better and more upbeat than she had earlier this morning at church, so that was a plus.

Sister Jewell watched Sally walk down the steps of her front porch and toward her cafe. Sad sad eyes, that girl. There's more to her story, no doubt about that. "God, I don't know all that's going on there with that young lady. I don't need to know everything, 'cause you do. What I do know, is she needs You and I trust You to see to her. Meet her needs, lift her spirits, encourage her, and protect her. Thank You, Lord, for your faithfulness."

Chapter Eighteen

ONE LOAF AT A TIME

Wherefore comfort yourselves together, and edify one another, even as also ye do.

Thessalonians 5:11

It was Monday afternoon, and Sister Jewell was taking round loaves of sourdough bread out of her oven and setting them on racks. As they cooled, she walked into her bedroom to put on her jacket and get her purse. She had some deliveries to make. It was a lovely fall afternoon and Snooky could use a walk. "Come on, boy, where's your leash?" Her eight-pound red poodle rounded the corner fast and furious, leash in mouth. "All right then, meet me in the kitchen." She took the loaves and placed each one into the paper bread bags she kept in plentiful supply just for these occasions, and out the door she and Snooky flew. First stop was Heather. "That dear girl will surely deliver her baby any day now. She has that *I'm ready look* about her," Sister Jewell told Snooky. "How the sweet thing is able to continue helping in the church office during the mornings, I have no idea," Sister Jewell concluded to her adoring companion.

Knock, knock, knock. Sister Jewell and Snooky waited on Heather's front porch. The door opened to the rounded smiling moon face of Heather. Sister Jewell thought pregnancy looked good on Heather. "Oh,

Sister Jewell and Snooky, how good to see both of you. Won't you come in?"

"No, shug, we have several deliveries to make this afternoon and so can't come in today, but I did want to offer my services to man the phone in the church office for you, temporarily, you understand. Surely, you need to be home resting at this late stage, instead of working mornings."

"Oh, my goodness! How thoughtful of you, Sister Jewell. Yes, I will take you up on your offer before too much longer."

"How 'bout now, young lady?" Sister Jewell scolded gently.

Heather chuckled, "Well, not just yet, but soon. Working in the mornings breaks up my day and helps the waiting for this baby go by faster, but I'll let Scott know of your generous offer. He'll be delighted." She opened the paper bread bag and breathed in deeply. "Oh, my, Sister Jewell, this smells heavenly."

Sister Jewell smiled lovingly at the young soon-to-be mother and said, "I hope you two enjoy it. Call me when you want me to start down at the church. Waving over her shoulder at Heather, Sister Jewell and Snooky headed for their next stop.

Walking into Dr. Mulligan's office, Sister Jewell saw Margaret sitting behind the front desk. "Good afternoon. Margaret, isn't it?"

"Yes, ma'am. How may I help you? I'm afraid Dr. Mulligan is out at the moment."

"That is perfectly all right; I'm here to see you," Sister Jewell said pointedly with a straight face that caused Margaret to stiffen anxiously with dread. "I've not had the opportunity to be introduced to you properly, so I'm taking matters into my own hands. I brought you some bread, dear, fresh out of the oven," smiling as she set the loaf on Margaret's desk. "I'm Sister Jewell; pleased to make your acquaintance," Sister Jewell said while extending her gloved hand.

Standing, Margaret shook her hand. Relieved, she smiled back into the amiable eyes of Sister Jewell. "Oh, thank you, Sister Jewell. You are so very kind. It's wonderful to make your acquaintance. Properly," she added with a wink.

"My pleasure, dearie. I think that youngster of yours will really like a slice of this bread toasted and buttered, at least I've yet to have any complaints. Tell him he is loved and keep that ornery Brother Fredrick in line for me." She laughed at her own joke and walked out the door of the office.

Relaxing, Margaret sighed, then smiled as she watched Sister Jewell march out the door with Snooky and on down the sidewalk. Reaching for the bread bag, she opened it and was met by the most delicious fragrance, tempting her not to wait until tonight for that toasted slice. She headed to the toaster oven in the office's back kitchenette.

Humming softly to herself, Sister Jewell and Snooky made their way down the sidewalk toward the Pierce's household. As she walked, she noticed the stranger she'd seen in church yesterday, coming her way. Immediately, a grating scraped across her spirit, and she knew. She recognized it as a warning, a flag, and began to pray under her breath as he approached. Snooky growled low as they got closer to the stranger. She stopped, nodding at the stranger, confronting him, face to face, a standoff, "How do you do, young man. I'm Sister Jewell."

"We know who you are," he rasped in what sounded like multiple voices.

Not surprised, Sister Jewell acknowledged, "Yes, well, I would imagine you do."

Restless, fidgety, and uncomfortable, the stranger was unable to look Sister Jewell in the eyes and seemed anxious to get away from her. "We've got to go. I'm sure we'll meet again," he said stiffly, tense, defying her even as he backed away.

"I feel certain we will, yes." Straightening up as best she could in an authoritative stance, Sister Jewell looked at him directly, boldly meeting his challenge and added fearlessly, "I'm praying, young man."

"We know," hissed the low, gravelly voices that rumbled out of the stranger's mouth as he hastily retreated as far away from Sister Jewell as he could possibly go. The stranger glanced nervously over his shoulder, anxious to put some distance between the two of them. There was always a remnant in every deployment he'd ever been on, he reminded himself, but he found it almost painful to be around this one. He wondered if he'd finally met his match.

Sister Jewell and Snooky climbed up the steps of the Pierce's front porch and rang the doorbell. Wiping her hands on her apron, Ruth opened her front door. "Get yourself in here, dear friend," Ruth giggled as she tugged on Sister Jewell's hand, helping her over the threshold.

Sister Jewell stepped through the front door, "I brought you some bread, shug," she said handing the bread to Ruth, "and was hoping to have a quick word." Sister Jewell was unusually somber.

"Well, of course, I'll put on the tea kettle."

"No, dear, that won't be necessary. Actually, I just want to pray with you about your small group meeting this Wednesday."

"Oh?"

"Do you have a moment?"

"For you? Always, come right in here. Oh dear, let me move those toys so you'll have a place to sit down," she said as she began to pile toys into the large basket sitting on the floor next to the sofa, kept there for just this purpose.

As soon as Ruth got a spot cleared of toys, Sister Jewell sat down on the sofa, and Ruth sat next to her. Without gossip, preliminary discussion, intro or any further conversation, in a fluid motion that seemed utterly familiar to both of them, they joined hands and promptly began to pray, one after another, back and forth and back again in conversational prayer that soon evolved into intense intercession for the upcoming Wednesday night meeting and those who would be attending, in particular, a certain stranger that had recently come to their town.

Chapter Nineteen
HOUSE TO HOUSE

...house to house, they never stopped teaching and proclaiming the good news that Jesus is the Messiah.

Acts 5:42

It was already hump day, Wednesday, and, as usual, it had gotten here before Ruth knew it. She seemed to always be meeting herself coming and going. She'd been busy putting a cake into the oven and tidying things up around the house a bit. Everyone was to arrive at about 6:00 this evening, the usual time. She hoped she'd have everything picked up, the cake iced, and the kids fed and upstairs doing their homework or off to youth group by the time everyone got to the house. It was always a challenge every week, but she and Henry had long ago decided it was worth it. As she worked, she thought about Sister Jewell's visit Monday. The assertive way Sister Jewell had prayed with her, sitting right here on her sofa, was nothing short of warfare. What had brought that on? What was Sister Jewell so concerned about that she'd made it a point to stop by and pray, intercede for her, her family, and the group that met in their home on Wednesday nights? Not that she and Sister Jewell didn't pray together often. They did, but this had been different. Intentional. Purposeful. Urgent. Really powerful. Whatever prompted

Sister Jewell's visit, Ruth was sobered by it. She'd learned long ago to pay close attention to Sister Jewell's leadings.

Ruth pulled a stuffed bunny out from between the cushions of her loveseat and tossed it in the toy basket. She then carried it, the sneakers, sweatshirts and all the other items she'd gathered upstairs to bedrooms or the attic playroom. As she climbed the creaking stairs she thought about their old house. She'd been so thankful to get it because of its size. It was huge and she and Henry had always wanted a lot of kids. This three-story house had enough space to raise their very large family, but it was also old and needed a lot of work, work that was sometimes, most of the time, impossible on their limited budget. Fortunately, she'd married a handyman, so every time the plumbing blew up or the electricity had a short, or any number of other problems that seemed to happen on a regular basis, Henry was usually able to at least put a band-aid on it and make it run a little bit longer without their being out a large sum of money. She didn't know how he did it.

What a good man her man was. God certainly blessed her the day she met Henry Pierce. What a moment that had been. She remembered it like it was yesterday. She'd just finished setting her canned preserves out at the county fair when she looked up from her table and saw him striding toward her booth. A ginger with freckles across his pug nose, she'd never seen a more handsome fella. Hair on the long side, he was wearing boots, Wranglers, and a vintage western cowboy shirt with snap pearl buttons down the front. Her pulse quickened when he stopped right in front of her table of preserves, tipped the brim of his Stetson, grinned from ear to ear and said, "Howdy, miss. I've been seeing you around town, and now you're here, I figure it must be fate. Wonder if you plan on being at the box social this evening before the barn dance?"

When she'd managed to stutter out that she would indeed be there, he asked her name and promised to see her later that evening, "...if you're all right with that, that is," he added.

Her deep blush had been the only affirmative response she'd been able to give him.

That night the bidding was fierce for her box supper. She had a good reputation around town of being an awfully good cook, and so several of the local fellas were vying for her fried chicken, as well as time with her, although she'd never admit that last part to herself. Finally, Henry won the competition. He bought her box, or in her case, basket.

Sauntering through the saw dust up to the front of the barn, Henry gathered his prize, offered his arm to Ruth, and together they'd found a nice tree outside the fairground's barn to sit beneath. Twinkly lights shone as he spread out the blanket she'd packed, and in concert they began to unload the feast she'd prepared earlier for this moment. At first Ruth felt completely tongue tied as if under some kind of weird spell, but before long she was telling Henry her life story, and he was going on about riding bulls, which she learned he did competitively. It was as if they'd known one another their whole lives. Finally, completely stuffed with as much of Ruth's tasty food as he could manage to hold to the point of nearly popping, Henry suggested they skip the dance and offered to give her a ride home. Then, as if the matter was decided, he began to reload her basket and fold up the blanket on which they'd been sitting. Arriving at his pickup, she couldn't help but giggle when she noticed he had to push aside boxes of her strawberry preserves to make a place for her to sit. It looked as though Henry bought every jar she had displayed on her table while she was away working as a judge in the pie competition. "I really like strawberry preserves," he muttered shyly under his breath as his face blushed beet red.

That was many years and six kids ago. Now she and Henry were like two ships passing in the night. Seemed like there wasn't enough time in the day. Oh, gosh, she'd better hurry; the kids would be home from school soon, and before she knew it, their small group would begin arriving.

Chapter Twenty

TWO OR THREE

For where two or three are gathered together in My name, there am I in the midst of them.

Matthew 18:20

That Wednesday evening, the stranger rang the Pierce's doorbell. Henry answered with a warm smile and welcomed him inside. As the two men took the few steps that led into the Pierce's living room, Henry asked the stranger if he'd like something to drink.

"Water would be perfect, thank you," said the stranger.

"Sure. You know, I've not caught your name."

"Amil," the stranger responded.

"Well, Amil, welcome to our humble abode. Make yourself comfortable. I'll go fetch you a bottle of water."

The stranger, Amil, sat down in the cozy living room and glanced up at the J.C. Penny's family portrait hanging on the wall facing him. One, two, three, six children. A lot of youngsters for anyone. He wondered how Henry and Ruth managed. It had to be tough making ends meet.

"Here you go." Henry handed him a bottle of water and sat down in the recliner across from him. "Where you from, Amil?"

"No place in particular. I've been hitching across the country for the last several years."

"I bet you've seen a lot. You could probably tell some fantastic stories," Henry spoke pensively.

You have no idea, Amil thought to himself, then said, "Yeah, I've seen a lot of countryside and have collected a few tales I could tell all right."

"Maybe you can share with the group later." Henry got up to answer the doorbell again and let in the next member or two of their small group. "Amil, I'd like you to meet Fredrick and Margaret. Fredrick can only stay a short time before he has to run off. He works with our youth at church on Wednesday nights, so he slips out of small group a little early each Wednesday."

"How do you do?" Frederick shook Amil's hand.

Soon, Matthew and Alice arrived, Ruth sat down, and Henry began, "Tonight we are continuing our discussion regarding Pastor's recent study of Ephesians 6."

Amil, the stranger, sat listening quietly, satisfied, pleased with himself and his progress thus far. How easy it was to become embedded in Christian assemblies or intimate little groups like this one. They were generally so open, welcoming and unsuspecting.

Outside the Pierce's home where the small group met, Dade drummed his fingers on the branch he was stretch out upon. Grinning like the Cheshire cat in *Alice in Wonderland*, he propped his head up with his free hand and watched. He was pleased with his boy's progress. *Good job, my pet*, he thought to himself.

Chapter Twenty-One

FOLLY

Folly is bound up in the heart of a child...
Proverbs 22:15

They'd been under the bridge by the crackling fire, smoking and talking most of the night. Their parents thought they were at youth tonight. They always thought they were at youth on Wednesday night. Jessie couldn't remember the last time he'd been to Wednesday night youth. He had no choice on Sundays because the whole family went together so he had to go to church, but Wednesdays were different. He was allowed to drive himself. Youth met separately from the adults, so the majority of the time, he drove himself right past the church and down to the creek and under this bridge where he met the others. "Here, put these drops in your eyes before you go home, Janie; it'll take the redness out, so your mom won't know," he said as he handed her a bottle of eye drops.

Taking the bottle Janie said, "Thanks," removed the cap, tossed her head back and was about to put a drop in her right eye when she stopped. "Why bother? I figure Mom won't be around; she's on a date and will probably stay with him tonight." She put the cap back on the bottle of eye drops and flung the small container back at Jessie.

"Whoa, gee, I'm sorry. That whole thing with your mom must be hard for you," said Jessie.

Looking at him, perplexed, Janie asked, "What? Why's that?"

"Uh, well, I meant your mom sleeping around."

"Shut up, Jessie. Don't talk about my mom like that," Janie pushed back, annoyed.

"Hey. Gosh, I'm sorry. Forgive me?" he grinned sheepishly.

"Sure. I'm sorry, too. It's just that, I don't know. It's always been like this. Guess I'm used to it. Mom's been trying to *find herself* ever since Dad split. I've pretty much raised myself seems like. I'm just thankful when she doesn't bring the guys to our home. Awkward, ya know?" Janie rolled her eyes.

"I can imagine. Well, actually, I can't imagine, and I suppose I'm glad I can't imagine," Jessie replied, digging himself a deeper hole.

"Your family seems pretty solid," Janie stated. It was pretty common knowledge that Jessie came from a good, stable family.

"Yeah, my folks are the salt of the earth. Good, decent, godly people."

"So why are you here if your life, your homelife is so wonderful?" asked Janie.

"Jarod and I have been best friends since kindergarten."

"Hey, dude, don't blame your bad choices on me," Jarod coughed out a large toke of smoke.

"Yeah, he's right. The main reason? I'll own it. I like to get high," Jessie admitted laughing.

Janie laughed too, "I see. Well, at least you're being honest." She stood up, brushed off her britches, and said, "Guess I'll see you tomorrow at school," then began walking up the embankment to her car.

"Yeah, see ya then," smiled Jessie, bleary eyed.

As Janie walked up the embankment to her car, she glanced back. Jessie was studying her thoughtfully and raised his hand in a silent farewell.

Jarod passed back the reefer to Jessie as he scooted closer, leaning toward his friend, "She's hot, man," he said, invading Jessie's personal space and speaking directly into his ear. "You got your eye on her?"

"Aaah, I don't know," said Jessie not wanting to be too transparent, even with his best friend. He took a drag and handed Jarod back the joint.

"Well, don't piddle around too long about deciding how you feel about her, or I'll scoop her up." Jarod inhaled deeply and held it.

Jessie considered his friend's admonishment while watching the taillights of her car drive away, down the bumpy country road, trailed by a cloud of dust. "Aah, okay."

At church, Stephen busied himself helping Brother Fredrick clean up the area where the youth had just met for their Bible study and refreshments. "Thanks, Stephen, I sure appreciate you staying late to help after Youth," complimented Brother Fredrick

"No problem, Brother Fredrick. Actually, I was wondering if I could talk with you about something," asked Stephen.

"Sure, buddy, let's sit over here." Brother Fredrick pulled two folding chairs together and set them up facing each other. He really liked this young man and felt great empathy for him. It'd been a struggle for Stephen since his mom died of breast cancer.

"Thanks. It's my dad again. He's drinking a lot, and I just don't know what to do anymore. He's never been the same since Mom died. It broke him," said Stephen as he sat in the folding chair.

"I understand how that can happen."

"Yeah, I know you do. That's why I thought you might have some ideas about how I can help him. Dad's a good man, Brother Fredrick; he just can't seem to find his way back, ya know?"

"I do know. My story is not exactly the same as your father's, I suppose. Betty left me, but let me tell you, just like your dad, Jim, I imploded. I spiraled around the drain for quite a spell. Questioned my masculinity, self-worth. I was filled with self-doubt, and I was so terribly, terribly hurt. I felt betrayed. I'd thought she and I would grow old together. I wondered why God would allow this to happen to me. Where had I gone wrong? I'd tried so hard to do everything right. The questioning is enough to drive a person crazy. So, I suspect that is some of what your dad is going through, the grieving, is not abnormal. Even the Lord cried when his friend Lazarus died."

"You don't have kids, do you, Brother Fredrick? I mean, the thing is, Linda and I lost our mom; we're sad, too, but Dad seems oblivious to our pain."

"I'm sure your dad is aware you're grieving, too. He's probably doing the best he can, Steve, but is just a little self-absorbed at the moment. He's so miserable he can't help anyone else right now. Not even himself."

"We need him, though. My sister really needs him. What can I do to bring him back to us, Brother Fredrick? What brought you back? I'm afraid I'm losing Linda, too. She's kind of gone off the deep end, it seems like."

"I noticed she wasn't here tonight. Stephen, I know it sounds cliché, but the best thing you can do is pray, love your dad, try to take up the slack where you can for your sister's sake, and did I mention, pray? Too often we underestimate the power of prayer. I've no doubt that the intercession of Sister Jewell literally saved my hide."

"I've been trying. Trying to pray. Honest. It's just tough to keep going on, ya know?"

"I do know. That's why you've got me, young man. I'm always available, ready to help support you in whatever way I can. Here, let me pray for you and your family right now." With that Brother Fredrick and Stephen bowed their heads and began to petition God to move on behalf of Stephen's family.

Chapter Twenty-Two

WRETCHED

"Satan has access to the domain of darkness, but he can only occupy those areas where mankind, through sin, has allowed him."

-Francis Frangipane

Walking with her head down, Lauren tried to avoid eye contact with any of the other students in the hall of Danport High. She angrily high-fived the school door under the lit-up exit sign, slapping the wood with the palms of both her hands, she burst out of the high school into the blinding sunshine, headed for home. Her clothing was bulky and layered. Her sleeves were always long to cover the slashes made by her cutting. As best she could, she tried to be unattractive, invisible, in hopes he'd leave her alone. So far, it hadn't worked. Walking up the steps to the side kitchen entrance of her house, she felt the hackles on the back of her neck rise upon hearing his voice from inside her family's home. He was on the phone, confident, jovial, and audible through the door. Turning the doorknob as quietly as possible, she thought maybe she might slip by him and sneak upstairs to her room. Maybe he wouldn't notice. Nope. Their eyes met. Dread. She knew that look. She could always tell. She knew he'd be bugging her tonight. A familiar foreboding washed over her, freezing her, until she could hardly move.

Strange sensation: she wanted to flee, but her legs wouldn't work. Besides, there was nowhere to run. This was his home.

Try to act normal, she thought, but what was normal? She wasn't sure. It'd started when she was eleven, so this was normal for her. Making herself a snack, she listened to the rest of his phone conversation.

"Got it, the church, six this evening. Understood. I'll be there," he finished before hanging up. Her father was an elder at the church, and tonight was their monthly meeting. Her family had always gone to church. In fact, they were there every time the doors were open. Perhaps the meeting would go long tonight, and if she pretended to be asleep when he got home, he might leave her alone this time. Before she and her dad could say anything to each other, her beautiful Mom, all bright and airy, blew through the kitchen side door with an armful of groceries.

"Here, let me help you with those, sugar; are there more in the car?" her dad asked her mom.

"Oh, yes, honey, that would be great. Thank you," said her mom as she smacked Daddy on his lips with a big kiss, "Hi, Lauren. How was school?"

"All right," mumbled Lauren.

"What's that? Darling, speak up, would you? And I wish you'd wash your hair; how long has it been? Really, I think it actually stinks or is that body odor? Oh, my gosh, are you not wearing deodorant? Why won't you wear some of those cute girly clothes I bought you? They're so much more feminine than what you have on. I declare, I can hardly tell you've even got a figure underneath all that garb you're wearing. Are you losing weight?"

Ignoring her mom, Lauren pulled her hoody up over her greasy hair and trotted upstairs with her snack. She knew Daddy was the reason Trish left the house as soon as she possibly could for college. She didn't really blame her older sister, but Lauren did sort of feel like she'd been abandoned, stuck with him.

Her mom was no help. Even though Lauren had tried repeatedly to talk to her about the nightmare in which she was living, her mother somehow remained painfully unaware. Or did she choose to be unaware? After all, how could she not know? Lauren had wondered if her mother chose not to acknowledge what was happening right under her nose, but how was that even possible? How could a mother choose not to see that her children were being victimized? Lauren wasn't sure, but whatever the logic to it, if there were any logic to it, the plain fact was she was on her own. She worried about Lola, her little sister, and how to protect her.

The headache that'd flirted with her all day had apparently followed her home and now slammed into her, coming on strong. Her forehead creased as it knotted up, tension snaked up the back of her neck, and her temple began to pound as if an ice pick were stabbing into it. Lauren knew it was probably just stress and tried to exhale and relax. Ignoring her snack, she left it on her chest of drawers, popped two aspirin, wet a washcloth with hot water, and covered her eyes as she lay down on her bed to wait it out. She intentionally let go, easing the tightness in her muscles one at a time, and focusing on the ticking of the clock on her bedside table. Just the ticking, nothing else. Such a peaceful rhythmic, nearly hypnotic sound. Tick, tick, tick. Soon she was deeply asleep, safe in the land of slumber. There is something about depression that is exhausting, making sleep easy to access, perhaps because of the desperate need for healing, protection, and the subconscious awareness that escape, any kind of escape, even in sleep, is critical.

Chapter Twenty-Three
THE INTERESTS OF OTHERS

Do nothing out of selfish ambition or vain conceit. Rather, in humility value others above yourselves, not looking to your own interests but each of you to the interests of the others.
Philippians 2:3-4

Jeannie complained to her mother, "She's so gross, Mom. Seriously, she smells bad. I don't know how she can even stand being in her own skin. Gah, I don't think she even shaves her legs!"

Ruth drove her daughter to Sonic, and they ordered their favorite, peach Sprite. It was *Happy Hour,* and so they got two large drinks. *Just what my hips need*, Ruth thought to herself as she smiled and handed the young man in the window his money. As Ruth and Jeannie parked the car in one of the few open slots, Ruth said, "There may be things going on in Lauren's world that we cannot even fathom, Jeannie."

"What, Mom, she can't even wash her hair? I mean, really?"

"What I'm trying to say is there may be things going on in her home life that we can't even wrap our heads around; things that are so foreign to us and the way we live, that we can't even grasp them. I just mean that I feel like there's more to her story is all."

"Like what?"

"Well, for this drastic of a transformation to have come over Lauren like it did, I just think it is significant. I remember her as a little girl, and she was adorable and she was always very clean, like Lola is now," Ruth pointed out. Poking her daughter in the ribs, she grinned and added, "She could probably use a friend."

Jeannie giggled, "Oh, Mom. Okay, I get it. I'll try to be just a little more sensitive."

"Just a little? Well, good. A little is better than none at all, I suppose."

"Alright, alright," Jeannie's voice lifted on the last alright. "I'll be a lot more sensitive. Maybe I'll even be a friend to her," she finished by rolling her eyes and taking a big slurp from her drink.

Chapter Twenty-Four
STIRRING THE POT

Let no corrupt communication proceed out of your mouth, but that which is good to the use of edifying, that it may minister grace unto the hearers.

Ephesians 4:29

Feigning ignorance, Amil asked questions about the preacher and the last sermon he'd delivered to the congregation at Community Church. "So, the preacher is new here, right? Do you like him? Do you like the way he preaches? The reason I ask is because I got pretty confused when he was talking about armor Sunday. We are to put on an armor, Brother Langley?"

"Well, no, not literally a metal suit, and yes, I suppose I like him all right," replied Richard Langley.

Shaking his head in insincere bewilderment, "Oh, I don't know, I just don't get it. It sounded to me as if he were saying we are to take up our shield. A shield? It's so confusing, and I'm not really sure what he said because he was sitting down, and I couldn't hear or see him clearly."

"Exactly. I agree. Yes. That is a problem. Sitting on the step so casually where he can't be seen or heard. Good grief, that's why we have a pulpit, so the speaker can stand up where we can see his face, and he can use the mic and all. It also sends a nice subliminal message for the pastor to be behind the pulpit, hidden, so only God receives glory."

"Pastor Scott is pretty young, seems like."

"Yes, he is young. Maybe he could use a few tips. Perhaps I'll speak with him."

"I saw that guy with all the kids, Henry, passing the offering plate, so I put money into it. Do you know where the money goes?"

"Well, Henry takes it back to the rear part of the church and counts it. It helps cover our church facilities' bills, pay our pastor and it supports a couple of missionaries."

"Henry seems like a good guy and all. I attended his small group Wednesday evening, and I like him, but how do I know he didn't put some of the money from Sunday's offering plate into his own pockets back there after he collected it all? I mean, he's got a ton of kids, his clothes are worn and he kind of looks like he could use some extra cash, if you know what I mean?"

Nodding his head, Richard's mind begins to twirl with unseemly possibilities.

Amil looked down, shaking his head, masquerading confusion while fully aware of the putrid seeds he'd just planted.

Chapter Twenty-Five

EXHORT ONE ANOTHER

But exhort one another daily, while it is called Today; lest any of you be hardened through the deceitfulness of sin.

Hebrews 3:13

It was Saturday morning, bright and early. Ben had already been dressed and ready to go fishing for an hour. He sat impatiently on the front porch waiting and waiting. *When will Brother Fredrick get here? It's taking forever,* Ben thought, as he flicked his feet back and forth beneath him.

He'd been too excited to eat his breakfast. Just when Ben thought he couldn't stand it any longer and couldn't wait another minute, Brother Fredrick finally pulled up in his old 1978 red and white Ford pickup. Pastor Scott waved at Ben from the passenger side of the pickup as Ben jumped out of the porch swing like there was a spring beneath him. He leaped off the porch and ran to greet the two men. Brother Fredrick scooped Ben up, laughing, as Pastor Scott looked on approvingly. Brother Fredrick said, "We stopped at the bait shop to pick up a few things, so we are running a little late, I'm afraid, Ben. Sorry if we kept you waiting."

"Aw, that's all right Brother Fredrick. What did you need at the bait shop? Can't we just use grasshoppers for bait?"

"Sure, but I wanted to get a knew floater or two and figured you'd need a doughnut. The bait shop always has a box of fresh doughnuts up at their checkout. If you can get beyond the fish smell, they're not half bad," Brother Fredrick laughed. "Look who I picked up along the way, Ben."

"Good to see you, young man," said Pastor Scott as he ruffled Ben's hair. "Thank you for inviting me to tag along this morning."

Ben's vocal volume was so over the top that he nearly roared at his pastor, he was so excited, "Oh, sure, Pastor. We are going to have a great time, aren't we, Brother Fredrick? We always have a super time."

"We really do, Ben. You better run in and tell your mama you're leaving," answered Brother Fredrick.

"Roger that," Ben popped off, running through the front door hollering for his mother.

Pastor Scott and Brother Fredrick glanced at each other grinning, relishing the little boy's excitement and enthusiasm.

Margaret appeared at the front door with Ben, "Well, I understand you men are about to head out. Ben, do you have your bug spray and sunscreen?"

"Yes, ma'am," Ben answered.

"All right then," Margaret leaned down to kiss Ben goodbye, "don't forget to apply them. Just packing them isn't enough, ya know," she smoothed his hair into place. "You behave yourself, young man, mind your manners and have a wonderful time."

"Roger that," Ben chirped.

"Bring us home some supper."

"Sure thing, Mom."

Brother Fredrick lightly punched Ben's arm and said, "Let's do this," and off they went.

Climbing into the old pickup, each one buckled up, and they took off down the road singing at the top of their lungs, *Gone Fishin'*, with Pastor Scott doing his very best Louis Armstrong imitation.

Standing on her front porch, Margaret watched as the men drove away until she lost sight of them. Smiling to herself, she turned to go back inside her house when movement to the side caught her eye. It was Sister Joslyn at her window across the street; she'd been watching them. In an effort to be neighborly, Margaret waved at her nosy neighbor but got no response, other than the abrupt curtain falling back into place concealing the local spy. Margaret shook her head, wondering how often she and Ben were under the surveillance of Sister Joslyn. Strange woman, Margaret thought to herself as she walked inside where she began to separate clothes so she could begin to do some laundry.

Chapter Twenty-Six

COUNSEL

Hear counsel, and receive instruction, that thou mayest be wise in thy latter end.

Proverbs 19:20

Monday, after getting the kids off to school, Ruth called her friend's office.

"Dr. Mulligan's office," Margaret answered cheerfully.

"Is Dr. Mulligan available?"

"Who may I say is calling?"

"Tell her it's Bugga-bear," giggled Ruth

"Bugga-bear? Uh, sure, one moment, please," Margaret put Ruth on hold.

"Ruth," Dr. Mulligan picked up almost immediately.

"Hey there, Helen. I was calling to see when you got back in town."

"What with the delays and all, it was really late. Our plane finally landed at around midnight. Made for a long day, that's for sure."

"I would imagine so. How was the conference? I'm sure you knocked it out of the ballpark and were a big hit."

"Ha, ha, hardly, but it all seemed to go off without a hitch. At least my breakout session was well attended and, hopefully, I was able to address some of the developmental issues and trauma our young people are facing these days."

"I'm sure you were amazing. Helen, would you possibly have time for lunch sometime this week?"

"If not, I'll make time. Let me look at my calendar. Hmmm, how does Thursday look?"

"Perfect. Want to beat the lunch crowd at Sally's, say about 11:30?"

"That'll work. See you then and, oh, uh, Bugga-bear, I'm glad you called. It's good to hear from you, old friend." Helen smiled hanging up the phone.

Dr. Helen Mulligan rose from behind her desk and carried the letter and file she'd been working on when Ruth called, back to her secretary, Margaret. "Margaret, if you could re-type this cover letter to DHS regarding the Downey boy's file, I've made a few changes. I'd like to confirm the trial date for the Egan custody case with Judge Calloway, and please reschedule my 11:30 appointment on Thursday; I've run into a conflict."

Chapter Twenty-Seven

SCHOOL DAYS

"It takes courage to grow up and become who you really are."
-E.E. Cummings

Jeannie bounced up to Lauren, "Hi, Lauren, I was wondering if you'd like to study together at my house after school today?"

Glancing around the door of her locker, pointing at herself, Lauren stammered, "Me? Are you talking to me?"

"Yep," Jeannie laughed, "we have the same literature class, and I could use some help. You free?" asked Jeannie nonchalantly.

"Uh, well, all right. O. O. Okay," Lauren stuttered, "I mean, if it's okay with my mom. I'll give her a call during lunch and ask."

"Great, I'll wait for you outside by the baseball diamond behind the school. We can walk to my house together."

Bewildered, looking suspiciously at Jeannie full in the face, Lauren wondered what the catch was, but muttered, "Sure."

Jessie nuzzled up to Janie's locker. "Hello, good looking; carry your books?"

"I've got 'em, thanks. Carrying a girl's books is a little archaic, isn't it?" Janie asked as she closed her locker door and started walking toward her fourth hour class.

Sprinting to catch up to Janie, Jessie slid up beside her. Walking together in the crowded hall he said, "I'm an archaic kind of guy," he laughed, "a real caveman. Ya know, ladies first and all that obsolete, old fashioned kind of stuff. So, I thought we might go on a date Saturday. You free?"

"Nah. Not interested. Nothing personal," said Janie.

"Ouch. Nothing personal? Really? That's kind of hard not to take personally," Jessie frowned, disappointed.

"I don't date, Jessie. Mom does enough dating for both of us. She's sort of soured me on the whole dating scene."

"Yeah, I get it, I guess. Well, maybe I don't. Janie, dating doesn't have to be anything you don't want it to be. Hey, I know, what if we just hang out?"

"What, under the bridge? Smoke?"

Jessie laughed uncomfortably, "Uh, no, I had a little more of an upgrade in mind. Maybe we could play chess or something?"

Puzzled, Janie glanced sideways at him and asked, "Chess? Are you kidding?"

"Prepare yourself to be dazzled, my lady," Jessie announced as he bowed theatrically with a flourish. "I am a renowned Grandmaster. In some parts of the world, I am known as Grandmaster Dubois."

"In your mind, maybe," Janie quipped. "Chess? Okay, yeah, maybe that would be alright."

"Fabulous. I'll be at your house Saturday evening around seven. You might want to do some stretches before our match."

"Right," Janie said skeptically, "We'll soon find out if you're all that. See you Saturday, Grandmaster Dubois. Game on."

Jessie cracked his knuckles and almost skipped down the hall to his next class. Sometimes it was hard to be suave and debonair.

Wearing black eyeliner, nail polish, ebony lipstick, and a cream-colored frilly poet's shirt, Blake, gothic to the core, strolled into Miss Holden's fourth hour with black bangs hanging in his shadowed eyes, his blocky dark boots, laced with silver bells, jingled with each tread. This was his first day at Danport High. His family had just moved here from NYC after his dad's promotion. The movers had no sooner unloaded his family's boxes than his dad was already flying off to another meeting. Talk about an absentee father, his dad could've written the book on that one. He was never around. Heads turned as Blake walked into the classroom and found himself a seat in the back, dropping his books midair like a bomb atop the desk with a loud bang. *I'm here, little ones*, he thought, as he glided smoothly into the chair.

Miss Alice Holden began calling roll. When she got to Blake's name, she paused and said, "Blake Williams?" as she looked around the room trying to locate him.

"Here," said Blake, standing and bowing while motioning with his hand in a flowery, twirling gesture from the back of the room.

"Welcome, sir," said Miss Holden.

"Thank you. Uh, Ms. Holden?"

"Yes?"

"Ms. Holden, if you wouldn't mind, my pronouns are they, them, their, theirs and themself. I prefer to be addressed accordingly."

"Pardon me?"

"I don't identify as either sex and would appreciate being referred to consequently," Blake replied as his new classmates' were suddenly very alert and began to take an interest, heads turned and looked in his direction and then back and forth amongst themselves, giggling.

"I see." Looking away, Miss Holden cleared her throat and began, "Today, class, we will be reviewing for Friday's test. Williams, since you're new here, this may require your catching up a bit, so hold on and pay close attention." She began writing an outline of study points on the white board behind her desk as she prayed silently for wisdom.

During lunch break, Lauren asked the school's secretary if she could use the office phone. Mrs. Rowder seemed surprised that Lauren didn't have her own cell phone; most kids her age did, but she said that it would be fine. Lauren dialed the number of her home's landline, hoping her mom would pick up. Surely her dad would be at work this time of day. The phone rang once, then twice, and then was picked up. The blood drained from Lauren's face and her breath caught when she heard her father's voice answering on the other end. She couldn't bring herself to ask him for permission to go. He'd never allow her to go to

Jeannie's home after school today anyway. It wasn't worth getting him worked up. Using both hands, shaking badly, she carefully hung up the phone as gently as she possibly could without saying a word into the receiver. Dejected, she crept out of the school office.

Mrs. Rowder was surprised to find Lauren gone when she turned back around to the phone from her computer screen. Strange girl, she thought, as she began to staple together the stack of forms the superintendent had requested for the meeting with the School Board, tonight.

Chapter Twenty-Eight

TATTLERS

And withal they learn to be idle, wandering about from house to house; and not only idle, but tattlers also and busybodies, speaking things which they ought not.

1 Timothy 5:13

Amil was busy pulling weeds out of Sister Joselyn's flower bed. He'd been pleased when she asked if he'd like some work landscaping and tending to her yard. He considered her a good connection, the perfect conduit for his purposes. Yes, he thought she would do quite nicely.

He hadn't been at it too long when he noticed she'd bustled down the front steps of her home and was now casting a very large shadow over his work area, making visibility difficult. He finally looked up from the turned over soil before him and said, "Good morning, Sister Joselyn. Do you need me somewhere else? The backyard perhaps?"

"Er, uh, no young man; actually, I was just popping out to see if you needed anything from me. Anything at all."

"No, ma'am. I think I've got everything I need."

"Oh, good. Good," she said, not moving to leave. "Where are you from, Amil?"

"Oh, ma'am, I'm from all over. I've been traveling for a long time. I pick up a job here and there along the way, earn a little money to tie me over, then I move on."

"I see. How do you like Danport so far?"

"I like it just fine," Amil smiled. "It seems like a great place to put down roots, raise a family."

"Is that something that interests you, Amil? Putting down roots and raising a family?"

"No, ma'am. I was born a traveling man. I get itchy and have to head on down the highway after too long in one place, but if I were thinking along those lines, Danport would be a great place to put down roots, like I said, and set up housekeeping."

"For the most part, yes, although some of those who've put down roots recently need to be uprooted like those weeds you're busy pulling, if you know what I mean?"

Amil recognized his open door and sidled up next to Sister Boland, confiding out the side of his mouth, "Well, it's interesting that you mentioned that ma'am. I have noticed that man, Brother Fredrick, spends a lot of time at that single mom's home. Becker? Across the street there?" He pointed across the street at Margaret's home. "Yeah, I think her name is Becker. Margaret Becker. He's there at all hours. I think I even saw him over there really early one morning before breakfast, as in...well, I shouldn't speak of such things in the presence of a lady like yourself, you being a woman of such refinement and grace," he looked down, masquerading embarrassment. He even managed to conjure up a blush.

Sister Joselyn nearly fell into Amil, she was leaning toward him with such intensity in her attempt to gobble up every tasty morsel of the juicy tale he was weaving for her. *She's so easy*, Amil thought to himself.

Amil went on, "Oh, and have you met that new family? The one that just moved here from New York City? The Williams? Well, their son wears eye liner. Eye liner!"

"Nooooo, oh, no. You have got to be kidding! Is he in our school? Corrupting our young people? This won't do at all," Sister Boland slavered hungrily.

"Yep, saw it with my own eyes. It's a real shame, isn't it?"

"Terrible. Just terrible."

"Well, Sister Joselyn, I'm on the clock so I better get back to work. I don't want to waste your money," said Amil, pleased with the kernel sowing he'd accomplished so far. He felt certain he would reap a blustery and fruitful harvest from this day's planting. Sister Joselyn was rich, fertile soil.

"I appreciate your honesty and integrity, young man. You are obviously a gentleman; a man who works hard for the money his employer pays him. Got to respect that."

Checking the water meter in the yard across the street, Dade looked on from beneath the large brim of his straw hat, smiling to himself with satisfaction.

Chapter Twenty-Nine

IRON SHARPENS

Iron sharpeneth iron; so, a man sharpeneth the countenance of his friend.

Proverbs 27:17

Ruth was nestled in the back booth, facing the café's window so she saw Helen when she flew through the door of Sally's, as if stepping over the threshold was the equivalent of crossing the finish line of a race. Ruth could see that Helen was in a flurry, whipped up in the hecticness that was the standard modus operandi for each of her days. Helen waved big at her friend Ruth as she hurried toward the back of the business. Ruth waved back in acknowledgement but was too late to catch her friend's attention. Helen was already steamrolling toward the booth where Ruth waited.

Ruth rose and greeted her dearest, oldest friend and confidant, with a hug, "Hey, there, stranger, how've you been?"

"To tell the truth, I'm meeting myself coming and going. Honestly, it's nice to have a lunch break and a little down time," Dr. Mulligan said as she took off her suit jacket, laid it over the Michael Kors handbag she'd positioned next to the wall in her seat across from Ruth and slid into the booth.

"I ordered us each a chicken salad sandwich, and there's your limeade," Ruth said, pointing to the tall yellow tinted glass of Dr. Mulligan's favorite iced drink, already resting on the dining table between them.

"Oh, thank you. Nothing hits the spot like a limeade; it really quenches a person's parched throat. It's a jungle out there," she laughed. "I think I could strike a match in my mouth right now, I'm so dry. Ruth, you know me so well," Helen concluded as she rolled her sleeves up to just below her elbow and drank deeply.

"Well, goodness, I would imagine so. Thirty years oughta get one pretty dog-gone familiar with the likes and dislikes of any person, especially my best friend in all the world."

Settled in at last, Helen looked at Ruth intentionally. "Have we really known each other that long, Ruth?"

"I figure so. Since kindergarten anyway," Ruth said thoughtfully.

"That's a long, long time, and we've not grown weary of one another yet." Helen took another sip from her drink, which seemed to coat the very insides of her stomach from the top all the way down. This limeade was long overdue and delicious.

"Oh, contraire, 'ole buddy, 'ole pal. At this point, you know way too much about me. The good, the bad and the ugly. The nitty gritty. All the details of my sordid life and then some. I can't possibly let you escape."

Helen laughed at Ruth's humor, "True, true, that street goes both ways, I'm afraid." She sat her limeade down pensively and looked across the table directly into the eyes of her oldest friend. "Okay, Ruth, what prompted this midweek meeting of ours? You've too many kids and way too frantic of a life to pause for a genteel luncheon date like this without an ulterior motive."

"Can't hide anything from you!" Not surprised, Ruth smiled, pressed her full lips together tightly, wondering how to continue, then added, "Yes, I wanted to visit with you about a little girl who's come across my radar. Helen, I'm really concerned about her."

Engaged, Helen nodded her head sympathetically. "Do I know her?"

"You may, that's why at this stage, I'd like to keep her name to myself, but she's in Jeannie's class. I just need some advice from someone I trust, who can help me understand what I'm seeing. What's going on, if anything is going on at all. She comes from a family in our church, a good family. Her dad is an elder, her mother seems loving and attentive. This girl used to be much like Jeannie, just a regular little kid, but then at some point after becoming a bit older, she seems to have almost quit bathing, her hair is usually unwashed, she wears layers of oversized clothing, and behaves beaten down, at least that's the only way I can think to describe it. Brow beaten," Ruth shook her head sadly. "Jeannie's been trying to reach out to her, to befriend her, but there have been some obstacles, one major obstacle being Jeannie's resistance to forming a relationship with this girl. Apparently, this young lady smells badly, and it's been kind of hard for Jeannie to get past that. Well, let me just tell you everything..."

Chapter Thirty

FRIDAY NIGHT LIGHTS

"My sport is marching band."

-Unknown

In most small towns, Friday night during the Fall means one thing, football. Danport is no exception. The drumline beat out the war cry of the Danport Lions as the team roared back onto the field with a minute left in the first half. On the north end of the field, the Pride of Danport, the High School's band was already lined up and ready to march out onto the field for their halftime show. Jarod and Jessie, both on the drumline, tapped out rhythms that for them had become second nature. Rat tat tatta tat tat, "GO!" Rat tat tatta tat tat, "FIGHT!" Rat tat tatta tat tat, "WIN!" Tatta tatta tat, "GO, FIGHT, WIN!" After a brief skirmish between the athletes on the field and one tackle later, the clock wound down, and it was half time.

As the football boys ran off the field and into their locker room, Jessie heard the stadium announcer raising his throaty voice, "And now, ladies and gentlemen, the pride of Danport, the Danport High School Lions Marching Band!"

That's our cue, Jessie thought to himself, establishing the tempo on his snare for *Na Na Hey Hey Kiss Him Goodbye* while marching onto the field at the pace and pattern that had won the band countless awards across the state this year. *He'll never love you, the way that I love you,* he sang in his head as he marched with tiny, practiced steps in the grid pattern that was burned into his memory. *So dog-gone willin', so kiss him, I wanna see you kiss him,* slide right, slide left, *I wanna see you kiss him, go on and kiss him goodbye, na na na, na na na,* march left, right, left, right, pause, sing, *na na na na, na na na na, hey hey, goodbye*, now just freestyle dance. This was Jessie's favorite part because he loved to dance. Now wave right arm slowly, starting up, then out and finally down.

The stadium full of football fans applauded politely, but Jessie knew the folks in the stands weren't here for the halftime show, even if the band had won way more state championships than the football team. He supposed sports would always be god.

After their show on the field, Jessie took his seat back in the stands with the rest of the band and watched the last half of the game. Part of the time he was thumping his instrument when directed by the drum major, and the rest of the time he was daydreaming about Janie. He could hardly wait for tomorrow night.

Chapter Thirty-One

DATE NIGHT

"Flatter me, and I may not believe you. Criticize me, and I may not like you. Ignore me, and I may not forgive you. Encourage me, and I will not forget you. Love me and I may be forced to love you."

-William Arthur Ward

Saturday night was finally here. He and Janie had agreed on 7:00 in the evening at her house. Her mom had a date and wouldn't be home, so it would be just the two of them. Jessie located his chess set, looked himself over in the mirror again and then expertly glided down the railing of the stairs. Before leaving the house, his mom asked if the two of them would be properly chaperoned at Janie's. Without actually saying yay or nay, he managed to slip out the door while squawking affirmative sounds, rationalizing his nothing burger response by telling himself it made his mom feel better. He wondered if all kids just instinctively knew how to squawk like that to reassure their parents.

Pulling up to Janie's home, he grabbed his chess set and climbed out of his Jeep. Walking up the sidewalk, he noticed the place was in need of a little tender lovin' care. He wondered how long it'd been since the grass had been mowed, the sidewalk edged, or the shutters painted.

Raising his fist to rap on the door, Janie opened it before his knuckles could connect with the wood. "Come in. I'm making us some nacho dip. Follow me." Like a puppy dog, he followed her into the kitchen.

The mouthwatering aroma of melting cheese mixed with Rotel filled the kitchen. Janie turned to him and asked, "Dr. Pepper, Coke, or Pepsi?"

"I'm a D.P. man, myself," Jessie said.

"Dr. Pepper it is," said Janie as she filled a giant tumbler with ice and then his favorite beverage.

"Man, that looks great! I can't believe how thirsty I am. I'm dry as a bone."

Janie laughed, "That's pretty dry. Why don't you take the chess set and your drink over there to that table," she pointed with her head. "You can set up the board while I finish up this dip," she concluded as she stirred the cheesy Rotel mixture that filled the crock pot.

"Sure," he said as he walked across the kitchen over to what he decided must be their breakfast table and began putting the chess pieces in position on his board.

Soon Janie joined him, setting two plates, a bowl of chips and the crock pot of hot thick sauce on the table between them.

"Awesome, Janie!" and he dove right in, covering the plate she'd brought him with chips, then allowing her to dip sauce all over the heap. As his stomach growled, he added, "I haven't eaten all day."

They didn't talk much as they settled into a thoughtful game of chess, weighing carefully each move and before they knew it, it was 11:00. That's when they heard the front door slam open with a bang.

"Excuse me," Janie said, rising to check on what might be going on in the living room.

Following her into the living room, Jessie had a bad feeling about what was coming next, and, as it turned out, with good reason. The two teenagers stood, looking on as Janie's mother was smashed against the wall next to the front door, pressed there by Duncan Barclay, Danport's local mechanic, who was kissing her passionately. She moaned, oblivious to the two teenagers who stood watching or, to Jessie's fascination, the grease that was a permanent stain under

Duncan's fingernails. Fingernails that were attached to the hands that now groped her lustily. Jessie was utterly appalled.

Horrified, Jessie knew his eyeballs had to be popping out of his face. He finally thought to close his gaping mouth, and with great effort, tore his stare away from the titillating lewd show right in front of him, a performance his mother would never have allowed as a movie pick, and yet this was a live production and unavoidable. He felt disappointment as he realized Mrs. Robertson had just thoroughly interrupted his evening with Janie. In fact, she'd brought it to a grinding halt.

"Harrumph, harrumph" Janie cleared her throat as Duncan turned his head, leering over his shoulder in their direction lasciviously.

"Oh, darling," her mother slurred, "you're still up," she giggled, unashamed.

"Yes, mother. This is my friend from school, Jessie."

With lipstick smeared all around her mouth, hair flared like Einstein, Janie's mother straightened herself. Smoothing her tight knit dress down into place over her shapely figure, she lifted her chin and swayed toward Jessie. Obviously, this wasn't her first rodeo. She was a pro and stumbled only once. Stepping up close to Jessie, he could see her blood shot eyes as she extended her hand. "Jessie," her breath reeked of alcohol and cigarettes.

"Ms. Robertson, it's a pleasure to meet you," Jessie said, nervously shaking her hand too zealously.

"Yes, well, I'm delighted as well," and with that she reached her other hand back for Duncan who was leaning against the door frame with his arms crossed across his chest. She pulled his collar toward her and down the hall they went toward what Jessie assumed was her bedroom.

Shocked, eyes wide, Jessie turned to face Janie and was surprised to be met by a hard, stoic countenance. That's when he realized this was just another night at the Robertson's for Janie. It didn't seem to have fazed her. She casually asked, "You okay?"

Spewing and sputtering words out with machine gun rapidity, Jessie spluttered, "Am I, am I, am I okay? Are you kidding me? Are *you* okay? How can you just stand there, Janie?"

"Stop. I think you'd better go."

"What? What? Go? Janie, I don't feel like I should leave you here tonight in this kind of environment."

"Who do you think you are? Mr. Goody Two Shoes? Like you can just bust into my life and sweep me out of *this kind of environment?*" She used her fingers to pantomime as she quoted his last four words. "Which night are you gonna pick to rescue me, Jeeeesssssiiiee, 'cause most nights are like this one. So, from which night are you gonna sweep me away and save me?"

"Janie, I'm sorry. I'm so sorry. I didn't know, okay? Well, I mean you'd told me but actually seeing it. It took me aback. I'm very sorry. Please forgive me."

"Just get out, Jessie. Go home to your perfect life, little boy," Janie spit, hurling harsh words as she pushed him out the door and slammed it shut behind him.

Jessie was halfway home before he realized his chess board was still sitting on Janie's breakfast table in her kitchen. *Checkmate, dude; you really blew it tonight.*

Chapter Thirty-Two

DEADLY ARROWS

They sharpen their tongues like swords and aim cruel words like deadly arrows.

Psalms 64:3

Her first poison pen letter would begin on this night. She'd never gotten over that meeting with Pastor and how dismissed and unappreciated she'd felt. She rehearsed what she should've said, what she wished she'd said, over and over again, reliving the conversation that day in his office. Her vexation mounted each time until she thought she would just burst. She desperately needed a release. Her mouth was almost salivating, as she took her favorite writing pen into her trembling hand, and with great excitement, began to vent. Not that she actually planned to mail the thing, no, she just needed to get a few things off her chest, and so she began to pour out her frustration. She told it like it was, each word the absolute truth, at least it was the truth from her perspective. Deep into the night she wrote and wrote until her hand began to cramp. She had so much to say. She was finally beginning to feel a great deal better when she wrote the last venomous sentence, concluding with the farewell sign-off: Most sincerely yours, A Concerned Congregant. There. She could exhale at last. This was good. This was really good. She might just mail this after all.

Chapter Thirty-Three

MY FLESH AND MY HEART FAILETH

My flesh and my heart faileth: But God is the strength of my heart, and my portion forever.

Psalm 73:26

Rinsing off the last coffee cup, Sally dried and stacked it. It had been a good day for the café. Saturdays were usually good and very busy. Wiping off the tables, she thought about her dad. He'd served three of his twenty-year sentence. Objectively, twenty years for murder didn't seem enough, but then when it was your dad who was serving the time, it seemed like forever. She'd never know for sure, she supposed. Did he do it or not? She wanted to believe he was innocent. She did believe he was innocent; however, there was this persistent nagging doubt down in her gut, but how was that even possible? Of course he didn't do it. He could never have killed her mother. He'd loved her. Sally had supported her dad throughout his entire trial. She'd sat right behind him day after day, declared his innocence to reporters and anyone who asked, but deep inside, she'd been plagued by doubt, doubt that she never spoke of.

Immediately after the verdict, she'd called a realtor and put their family home on the market. Next, she'd begun to box things up. Finishing all that, later that week she'd left town early one morning, while it was still dark, when no one was awake to see her go. After successfully slithering out of her hometown unnoticed, her plan had been to start fresh, and so she'd moved to Danport where no one knew her or her story. Since opening the café, she had pretty much worked 24/7. It wasn't too bad. After all, it provided a distraction, which she desperately needed. It took her mind off things; off the grief she felt over losing her mother and the confusion of having her father convicted of murdering her mother. In other words, the long hours of constant hard work gave her no time to fret and wore her out to the point of collapse each day, so it kept her mind from obsessing about the current state of her life.

She took the grill brick and began scrubbing. A whiff of sulfur rose from the griddle, unwelcome, the strong odor met her nose. She didn't know if she'd ever start feeling like her old self again.

The night her mother died, she'd been at the library like usual, working on her thesis again. She'd been in her final year of graduate studies and had already invested four months on her dissertation. She'd become a regular at the library and was at this particular table most nights. This was her table, her spot. Like people become accustomed to a certain pew in church, she'd become comfortable with this location in the library. She wasn't beyond asking people to move if they were sitting at her table because she wasn't sure her thoughts would flow and come together if she were seated anywhere else.

She was just beginning to see the light at the end of the tunnel. Looking high and low for an article on geomorphology, she was on her hands and knees under the worktable, hair piled high on her head, pencil clinched between her teeth when she noticed shoes standing by the overflowing wastepaper basket next to the table where she was all spread out and had been working. The police had found her. As some of her hair fell loose and into her eyes, she'd crawled out from under the table and was greeted by Ronny and Joe, the local cops. She knew them well, had gone to school with them and had even dated Ronny. She'd always thought he was so handsome. She wasn't sure why they'd quit seeing each other. Probably her fault; she'd gotten too busy trying to finish school. Why couldn't he look her in the eyes? Why couldn't any of them?

It was odd to see Pastor Jim with them. Then it hit her like a meteorite, and she knew before he opened his mouth, something terrible had happened.

"Sally, honey, we've got some bad news; there's been an incident," Pastor Jim began, "it's your mother. She's..."

"What?" screamed Sally, tears stinging her eyes.

There were other students scattered around the second floor of the library who had become familiar with Sally over time in that they generally nodded a good evening to one another before each setting up their prospective study camps, night after night, in their respective corners of the library. Those students now jolted from their work and turned their heads sharply, curious, wondering what the ruckus was all about. Some stood to get a better look and whispered amongst themselves.

But at that moment for Sally, it was as if there were no other students on the floor with her. The walls closed in around her tightly as if she and the three men in front of her were the only ones in the whole world. She couldn't breathe or see anyone else, and her ears began to buzz loudly. Pastor Jim put his arm around her shoulders. "Sally, she's gone, your mother passed away, sweetheart."

Sally pushed him away and looked at him incredulously, her mouth falling open in utter disbelief and shock. Skepticism creased her forehead. "How's that possible? I just left her Sunday. We had dinner together. I had to help her eat, sure, but she was fine, she was fine. Was it, was it..."

Ronny stepped closer, gently touching her arm. "It looks like she may have been murdered, Sally. We've arrested your father."

Sally felt as if the wind had been knocked out of her. Suddenly lightheaded, a black veil fell over her vision, her eyes rolled back into her head, and her knees buckled. She was instantly a noodle, but Ronny managed to catch her before she crumbled completely to the floor and carry her out of the library. Neither of the other men questioned Ronny when he told them he'd take Sally to her apartment and stay with her. Left behind in the library, the other two men carefully gathered up Sally's books and study material, storing it in her backpack. Pastor Jim offered to drop it by her place in the morning when he checked in on her.

Laying Sally on the sofa of her apartment, Ronny quietly began to pray as he covered her with the throw his mother had crocheted. He remembered how close he and Sally had once been and wondered how he'd let her slip away. His mother reminded him often enough that he'd messed up by not marrying Sally, but somehow, it just hadn't worked out. Maybe it just hadn't been the right time. Turning the flame on under a kettle of water on her stove, he found the tea bags, remembering she liked Earl Grey. It was gonna be a long night.

Chapter Thirty-Four

IT ONLY TAKES A SPARK

> *Likewise, the tongue is a small part of the body, but it makes great boasts. Consider what a great forest is set on fire by a small spark.*
>
> James 3:5

Jessie and his family got to church just as the first hymn was beginning. He took off his hat as he entered the sanctuary and sat down in the pew his family always occupied on Sunday mornings. He looked around the congregation hoping to see Janie. He'd tried calling her several times after their disastrous night of chess, but she wouldn't pick up, so he texted her trying to apologize, blathering on about how he hoped to see her in church. She was definitely ghosting him. Guess he couldn't blame her. He couldn't believe how ill equipped he'd been to handle the nightmare that was her life. Obviously, he lived a very sheltered existence. He felt embarrassed by his inadequacy. The strange thing about everything that had happened was that somehow, he ended up feeling the weight of responsibility he should've been feeling all along as a believer, to be a godly influence. It was true that he was a Christian with a great home life, but obviously, he'd been taking a lot for granted. Meeting someone like Janie, who wasn't as fortunate as he had been all his life, had been a real eye opener. It made him feel deep conviction and remorse for having taken so many things as just a given. No more.

Pastor Scott stood in front of the pulpit as Henry walked forward with the offering plates, "Henry, would you like to pray?"

"Sure, Pastor," Henry responded as he turned to face the congregation and bowed his head, "Father God, we bless You and give You praise for the many ways You care for us and meet our needs. Malachi 3:10 promises us that if we bring our tithes and offerings to the storehouse, You will open up the windows of Heaven and pour out more blessings than we are able to receive. We trust that Your word is true, that You are not a man that You should lie. If You said it, then You will do it. Thank You, Father. In Jesus' Name, Amen."

Richard rolled his eyes. What a hick, he thought with disdain, watching Henry closely as he carried the offering plate to the back of the church. He leaned over to the person next to him and said, "What's the deal with the pastor? Why won't he stand behind the pulpit. He should keep a closer eye on that offering plate. I mean, does anyone really know how much money we take in each Sunday? Who's making sure that cowboy isn't dipping into the pot? With all those kids of his, I'm sure he could use some extra cash. Look at him. Did he get his clothes at the mission house?"

At first, startled upon hearing all of this, the thin person next to him held a pinched expression and just nodded, but Richard had ignited a spark. With little effort, Richard had managed to successfully plant questions in the mind of his neighbor in church that morning. A spark that would lead to a forest fire.

Chapter Thirty-Five

BATTLES

"Everyone you meet is fighting a battle you know nothing about. Be kind. Always."

-Brad Meltzer

Church let out and the congregants poured out into the front lawn. Many small groups of people stood about visiting before going home. Walking up to Lauren, Jeannie had a little talk with herself again for the hundredth time, regarding the value of lovin' on Lauren, even if she did look like she'd been sleeping under a box on the street for a month. "Hi, Lauren, how're you doin'?"

Lauren looked down and mumbled, "Oh, uh, doin' all right I guess." Pulling her collar up closer around her neck, she looked about warily.

Jeannie followed her glance and saw Lauren's family in the distance, her father looking their way. "Hey, I was sorry you weren't able to come to my house after school the other day. I wondered if you'd wanna come home with me for lunch today?"

"Mmm, I don't know," Lauren looked doubtful, "I'd have to ask my mom."

"Sure, I get it."

Turning clumsily, Lauren lumbered over to where her family stood and spoke to her mom. Her mother burst into a bright smile, thrilled that her daughter might actually be making a friend. Attempting to straighten Lauren's hair, she nodded affirmatively.

Just then, Lauren's Dad stepped up between them. Shaking his head no, he grabbed Lauren's upper arm tightly and began to firmly guide her to their car. Looking over her shoulder mournfully, Lauren caught Jeannie's eye as her mother clucked about, gathering Lauren's little sister, and ushering her quickly behind her husband and middle daughter to their family's car.

Well, she'd tried, Jeannie thought, as she skipped up to her family. Wait 'till her mother heard about this one. Lauren's dad was such a jerk. What was with him, anyway?

Chapter Thirty-Six

REACHING OUT

"When one reaches out to help another, he touches the face of God."

-Walt Whitman

After the church service, Sister Joselyn could hardly wait to begin digging around the topsoil with a more thorough investigation of the seeds of gossip Amil had strategically planted. Nice young man, that Amil. So respectful. Excellent gardener. In Sister Joselyn's rush, she nearly tripped over Henry's little one. Or one of them anyway; he had so many. Why couldn't he keep his brood in check? Someone should really speak with him about those sticky little rug rats. Gad, how many were there? Sister Joselyn gasped. *There he is! That new kid. Williams. From New York City. Lord, have mercy. Amil was right; he does have his eyes lined!*

About that time Stephen walked up to the Williams' boy, extended his hand, and introduced himself, "Hi, I'm Stephen."

Taking Stephen's hand and shaking it, the surprised young man, dressed in total black, replied, "I'm Blake. Blake Williams."

"Have you guys settled in, or could you use a hand? I don't have practice tomorrow after school. I could stop by your house, do some hoisting and lifting," Stephen grinned.

Blake looked genuinely surprised, but then composed his facial expression, "Sure, that would be great."

"Okay. See ya tomorrow afternoon then about 3:30," and Stephen sauntered off.

Blake's eyes never left Stephen. He followed his exit curiously. *What's he up to?*

Aghast, Sister Joselyn huffed and puffed, making a mental note about what she'd just witnessed with her own eyes; this might inspire another letter. She rushed out the side door where she was thrilled to bump into her best friend and promptly spilled her guts. By the time she got to her home, she was in a real dither; her angst had risen to a feverish pitch. She plopped down at her writing desk, took out her favorite writing pen, and began her next letter. This letter would be a masterpiece. *Dear Stephen, who do you think you are? John the Baptist? Moses? No. You are the son of a drunk. A drunk for crying out loud. Maybe you should remember that and worry about things at home instead of associating with low life creatures who've crawled out of the gutters of New York City. That creature wears eyeliner and nail polish for crying out loud. What is that thing? A girl or a boy? Who knows? An abomination, of that, there is little doubt. Meanwhile, your sister is a train wreck...*

Chapter Thirty-Seven

SUNDAY

"Sunday clears away the rust of the whole week."
-Joseph Addison

Pastor Scott helped Heather down the steps of the church, and they walked the short distance together to their home. Her hand rested on his arm as they talked about their baby's hiccup episode during the Lord's Prayer that morning. It had been hard to keep a straight face as her belly jostled about with a steady beat. "I'll tell ya, Scott, I just almost burst out laughing."

Scott smiled and patted her hand. "It won't be long now, shug. Are you getting excited?"

"I suppose I am and a little nervous, I gotta admit. I think maybe it's the not knowing. I'm not sure what to expect."

"You mean during the actual birth?" Scott probed gently.

"Exactly," Heather exhaled, "We'll have plenty of help once the baby is here, but the birth is something you do pretty much alone, ya know? Oh, I hope that doesn't hurt your feelings; I know you'll be there, the doctor and nurses will be there, but even so, it's still all on me. Does that make sense?"

"Perfect sense. Hmmmph, of course your pastor would remind you that you are never alone."

"I know that, Pastor, yes, I'm aware that He never leaves or forsakes me. I'm just being real, talking like a flesh and bone human-being for a minute," she giggled as she punched him.

Thank You, Father, for this one. What a gift, Scott prayed silently as they opened the door to their home and stepped in.

Jeannie set the table as she jabbered on and on to her mother about Lauren's weirdo father. "Really Mom, you should've seen him. I mean, what a jerk."

Ruth looked concerned as she began to pour tea into the ice filled glasses Jeannie had already set by each plate.

"I wouldn't be surprised if he bruised Lauren's arm. He was practically forcing her to get in their car. What's his deal anyway? Mom, if you could've seen the look on Lauren's face and the way her mother started darting around like a chicken with her head cut off." At this Jeannie puffed herself up royally and said haughtily, "It was as if the king had spoken, and all his peasants were rushing to comply. I mean, who does he think he is anyway?"

Shaking her head, Ruth said more to herself than to Jeannie, "I'm not sure what, but something's amiss there."

"What, Mom?"

"Oh, nothing, shug; go tell everyone we're ready for them. I'll get the roast out of the oven." Ruth turned to go back in the kitchen. As she did, with a heavy heart that ached for Lauren and her family, she began to pray, *Father, I don't know what's going on there, but you do. God, help Lauren. Show me what I can do, or if I should do anything. Fill me with Your wisdom and discernment...* at just that moment the tornado that was her family, with hollers, laughter, and pounding feet, arrived in full force around her dining table. Her prayer time abruptly interrupted, Ruth smiled in surrender and carried the platter of roast, potatoes and carrots through the door and set it in the middle of their long table as she thought about how pleasant it was to have an afternoon where they could actually all sit down together over a nice meal.

Positioning herself at one end of their dining table, Ruth smiled at Henry who sat at the other end and asked, "Jeannie, would you go get the carving knife for your father?"

Henry returned her smile as unspoken words of love and gratitude passed between them.

Chapter Thirty-Eight

CAN'T TRUST THAT DAY

"Monday, Monday, can't trust that day. Monday, Monday, sometimes it just turns out that way..."

-John Phillips

It was Monday morning, and Brother Fredrick stopped by to pick up Ben. He'd promised to take Margaret's little man to school this morning, but first they'd planned on getting a donut at Sleeps. The morning was just breaking as Margaret opened her front door, still in her bathrobe, explaining that she was running late for work. Brother Fredrick smiled, assuring her that it was no problem and asked if Ben was ready.

"Surely, he's just about ready. I can't imagine what's keeping him. I'll go put a fire under him. Come in, come in Fred," said Margaret as she stepped aside to make room.

Fredrick stepped in as Margaret hollered to Ben, "Benjamin. You need to hurry, honey. Have you brushed your teeth? Brother Fredrick is here for you," she finished, closing her front door before rushing to Ben to see if she could get him to hurry along.

When Margaret found her son, he was standing in front of the bathroom mirror combing his hair. He'd parted it on a different side then usual and was shaping it in a style she'd never seen on him before. Suddenly, she recognized the style her son was trying to emulate. He was combing his hair just like Fred's. Her eyes instantly misted over as her heart warmed toward the man who'd become so important to them both.

Fifteen minutes later, Sister Joselyn opened her front door, stepped outside, and picked up the newspaper from her front yard, all the while keeping one eye on Margaret's house across the street. Of course, it was at that exact same moment that young Ben was finally ready so that he and Brother Fredrick could leave the house for school. Sister Joselyn was on high alert when Margaret's front door opened across the way and out stepped Brother Fredrick with Ben, Margaret standing in the background, in her bathrobe.

Clutching the newspaper to her breast Sister Joselyn sputtered, "My heart, my heart," under her breath, "Dear Lord, is Margaret really in a bathrobe? So brazen. Oh, she's sultry. Sly, that one, dripping seduction. Poor, poor Brother Fredrick; how he's fallen. Fallen! She's loose; that's all there is to it, and she's trapped him. That's obviously what's happened here. How could he help himself? What man could? Oh, my, was he there all night? He's just now leaving her lair and herding that scrawny little mongrel of hers away from her den of depravity." Sister Joselyn mumbled to no one as she openly gawked. She had to admit it; Amil had been right again. The proof was in the pudding. She could see it with her own eyes, right there in front of her, for God and the whole world to see.

Slapping her wrinkled newspaper against the palm of her hand, she shook her head in disbelief as she walked back into her home. As soon as she got inside, unable to restrain herself, she picked up her phone and speed-dialed the number of her best friend. Her friend had barely answered the phone before Sister Joselyn took off regurgitating the whole story of what she'd just seen. Without even taking a breath, she relayed her version of what had just happened across the street.

Stephen waved at Jeannie in the hall. "Hey, you. Now that coach is laying off on early morning practice for a while, I thought we could maybe start back with our early morning prayer meetings, beginning maybe tomorrow. You free?"

"Sounds great. I've missed those. I'll be there. Say about 7:30 around the flagpole?"

"Perfect. Say, I was hoping you might invite Lauren."

Rolling her eyes, Jeannie said, "This must be God."

"What?" Stephen looked at her quizzically.

"Everybody's been trying to get her into my world, meaning my mom. Now you. Okay, sure, I will invite her."

Without judgement, Stephen responded, "Thanks, Jeannie; that'll be awesome."

Turning, Stephen saw Blake. "Hey, Blake. Say, I wondered if you'd like to join us in the morning. About 7:30 at the flagpole?"

Jeannie couldn't help but be surprised by Stephen's boldness. Her surprise was followed by admiration and then inspiration. She decided to follow suit. She would do everything she could to get to know Lauren and become her friend.

Blake responded to Stephen's invitation to meet at the flagpole, "Dude, thanks, but I'm not that patriotic. Doesn't sound like something worth getting out of bed for. What do you do? The Pledge of Allegiance and the Star-Spangled Banner?"

Laughing, Stephen said, "No, nothing like that. The flagpole is just a conspicuous place for us to all meet here on the school campus. We may step over from there to the picnic tables or some other area after we get started."

"Started?"

"Not gonna lie to you, friend. We sing praise songs, read scripture, and pray. You'd be very welcome to join us. Seven-thirty tomorrow morning if you decide it is worth getting out of bed for," he ended with a wink. Blake walked off, perplexed, wondering, what does that holy roller want with me? Duh, Blake. He wants to *save* you. Isn't that always their mission? Yes, and save me from what? Nevertheless, he had to admit that there was something about this guy Stephen that was genuine, so Blake thought why not? Yeah, he might just go. Sure, he'd get all dolled up, go in the morning, and see if he could rattle the pretty little cages of these precious flagpole saints. This might just be fun.

Jeannie bounced up to Lauren, "Hey, friend."

Startled, Lauren shrunk into her locker. "Oh, hello, Jeannie. I'm sorry it didn't work out for me to go home with you yesterday after church. It would've been nice."

"No prob. Just wanted to let you know that we are all meeting tomorrow morning, 'bout 7:30, around the flagpole. Hope you can make it."

"What's going on?"

"We're just having a brief devotional time. I figured since your dad is an elder at church and it's on your way to class; he might let you come to it?"

"Uh, maybe. I'll see," Lauren whispered as she looked away.

Catching a quick glimpse of crimson, Jeannie touched Lauren's shoulder, "Hey, Lauren, you all right?"

"Sure. Yeah," Lauren's back remained toward Jeannie.

Jeannie gently turned Lauren around to face her, noticing immediately that Lauren's eyes were swollen as if she'd cried all night. Her face was splotchy. Her chin and neck were scratchy red. If Jeannie didn't know better, she'd say that was whisker burn all over Lauren's neck. How odd. Jeannie didn't know of anyone Lauren was dating. With whom had she been making out enough to get that whisker burn? "Hey, Lauren, what's going on?"

"Nothing. I'll try to be there in the morning, Jeannie. Thanks for the invite," Lauren mumbled over her shoulder barely audible as she rushed off, retreating into her first class, all the while wishing Jeannie would leave her alone and stop rocking the boat. Why was Jeannie trying so hard to be her friend? She had enough trouble to deal with already.

Pulling up into her driveway, after a long day at work, Margaret got out of her car, walked up to her front porch, and checked her mailbox. Standing there on the stoop in front of her door, she flipped through the junk mail and bills, noticing a letter addressed to her that had no return address.

Unlocking her front door, she walked into her home. Laying her keys on the entry table, she flopped down into her favorite chair and began opening her mail, finally getting to one with no return address. Opening the envelope, she pulled out the letter from inside. The script was scorching, and her eyes began to mist up as the read the hateful content. For some reason she couldn't tear her eyes away; she couldn't stop reading the toxic words. It was like staring at roadkill; she was unable to quit. Who would send such a foul thing? There was no signature. No clue as to who had sent it. She'd never read anything so contemptible, so evil.

Sneaking a glance, peering out through her window at Margaret's house across the street, Sister Joselyn had a smirk of satisfaction on her pudgy face. Her cheeks were rosy, flushed with pleasure as she closed the curtain and tucked its folds back into their proper place. She exhaled a deep cleansing breath. My goodness, this was liberating. She was unable to find the words to describe how much gratification her new *hobby* brought her. She felt utterly free. This was wonderful. Glorious. This was great. Addictive. She had to have more. Quickly moving her large frame over to her writing desk, she pulled out her pen and paper and began once again to write. *You are an oily, pocked face, homely bore. Bore. That best describes you. Your sermons are so dull and monotonous, I can hardly stay awake. You know nothing about life, the trials, and tribulations most of us face. You are such an innocent. A child in need of maturity. You are so juvenile. How can you expect to minister properly to the people in your congregation? These people have lived real lives and have real problems. And that wife of yours, what did you ever see in her? She makes me gag. She is as big as a barn and so milk toast plain....*

Behind Sister Joslyn, lounging on her pink and blue flower print sofa, Dade popped a grape into his mouth and then plumped up one of her lacy pillows and tucked it behind his head. He then kicked his feet up, elevating them onto the other end of her sofa. With one arm behind his head, he raised the bony pointer finger of his other hand to the slimy, muscular organ of his black tongue. Once moistened, he tapped his crooked digit to a particular spot in the air above his head while making a sizzling sound. Ssssssss. He was hot. Oh yes, he was on fire. Truly, his master's plan was all coming together nicely. He just adored when all the puzzle pieces began to fall into place. He'd soon have a good report to relay to his lord. As he meditated on the account he would deliver, he closed his eyes, imagining himself basking in the approval of his sovereign. Time for a little nap, he thought contentedly. This couldn't have gone better if he'd overseen the whole affair himself. Oh, he had. Yes, he'd supervised it from the very beginning, he thought merrily. Things were moving right along. Right on schedule. Everything was going very well. Very well indeed. Fully relaxed, Dade began to snooze.

By the time Danport High's lunch period arrived, Stephen and Jeannie had printed off a few fliers in the school office, advertising tomorrow morning's meeting around the flagpole. It helped to know the school's office secretary when you were trying to get something done in a hurry. As kids were settling in, around the cafeteria tables, Stephen and Jeannie handed out their leaflets. They were met with every kind of response imaginable: some were receptive, and others were thoroughly annoyed.

Willie rolled his eyes and then wadded up the flyer Stephen had handed him into a ball and threw it at Susie just across the table from him, hitting her in the head, producing the desired effect, her snarl.

Heedless, Stephen sat down next to Jeannie, positioning his lunch tray on the table in front of him. "I think we might have a pretty good turn out in the morning. Got any idea where we should begin tomorrow?"

"I'll leave the lesson up to you this week and bring my guitar for a few songs. We can switch back and forth. Next week I can bring the message if that sounds all right to you?"

"Sounds like a plan," Stephen said, crunching into his buttered cornbread and scooping up a big spoonful of stew.

Alice Holden had been a teacher at Danport High for about ten years, and during that time, she'd learned that you could often see the writing on the wall. Kids generally set their course as youth. Once set, it was then awfully hard for them to change paths. It wasn't impossible, but it was really tough. Alice, watched from over by the exit doors of the cafeteria, thinking about what good kids Stephen and Jeannie were. She knew it hadn't been easy for Stephen, losing his mother and then having his dad struggling so with that loss. Despite all that, he seemed to be on the right track. She did worry about his sister, though. She looked across the noisy cafeteria at Stephen's sister, Linda, and shook her head in concern. It didn't help that, Willie; Matthew's little brother was part of that troubled group. What would it take to get their attention?

Linda sat with her group: Jarod, Susie, and Willie. Linda was embarrassed that her brother Stephen was so out there. He was such a radical. She'd watched from the side of her eye as he handed out his little fliers and then sat down next to Jeannie, the good girl. She appreciated that no one at her table harassed her about her brother. Oh, my gosh. Were Stephen and Jeannie bowing their heads to pray? Linda's face blushed beet red as she looked straight ahead and attempted to appear nonchalant and oblivious to the awkward scene her brother was making.

Chapter Thirty-Nine

SEE YOU AT THE POLE

For I am not ashamed of the gospel of Christ: for it is the power of God unto salvation to everyone that believeth...
                                                    Romans 1:16

Tuesday morning, Jeannie grabbed her guitar and was waiting at the school's flagpole bright and early. She'd been glad that she and Stephen had taken a few moments yesterday to pray about this morning, before lunch period ended. Her heart had begun to feel very heavy for Lauren, which surprised her, since initially, she could hardly stand her. Now she was hoping she'd show up this morning.

Stephen arrived next and grinned brightly, "Good morning, beautiful," he said as he handed her a styrofoam cup of coffee.

"Thanks, Stevie!"

Other kids began arriving and gathering around the pole, when, preceded by loud heavy metal banging, Blake's car rolled up. Gracefully uncoiling himself from the driver's seat, he stood tall in black platform boots with his blousy lacy shirt, complete with a skull brooch and shiny black leather pants, with silver chains on each hip. He was in full gothic makeup, piercings, rings on fingers with sable nail polish, hair dyed inky and hanging down in his heavily lined eyes.

Thinking himself at the height of shock and awe, Blake was surprised that Stephen seemed unfazed as he approached. "Hey, there. Glad you could make it." Stephen welcomed him by shaking his hand and then walked alongside him toward the group gathered around the pole.

Slipping up to the group, but staying behind the others, hoping no one would notice, Lauren materialized just as they were about to begin. She cautiously stayed in the background. Sensing Lauren's discomfort, Jeannie was careful not to rush her as was her impulse. Jeannie thought how different their lives obviously were. Hers was all sunshine and roses, so she tried to be sensitive to Lauren, whose world was apparently nothing like that.

Stephen opened by greeting everyone, and then Jeannie began leading them in a few songs. After Stephen's brief devotional, he closed in prayer, and it was over. Quick, simple, no big deal and yet Blake felt what? He wasn't sure, but something. Enough that it bugged him. He couldn't wait to get away from there.

Lauren couldn't stop crying. She ran to the bathroom and into a stall, hoping no one had noticed her breakdown. How could such a simple little meeting like the one this morning get her so shook up. Lauren heard someone come into the bathroom, rip off paper towels, and run some water over them. Minutes later, Jeannie was handing Lauren wet paper towels under the bathroom stall door, "I'm not gonna bug you, Lauren, but I want you to know that I'm your friend, I'm praying for you and if you need to talk, I'm available," and with that she left Lauren alone in the bathroom.

Chapter Forty

COMMONALITY

"With old friends, you've got your whole life in common."
-Unknown

Sally rushed to catch the phone, "Sally's Café," she answered breathlessly.

"Hey," said the deep familiar voice on the other end.

"Ronny," screamed Sally excitedly, "How on earth have you been?"

"Well, that's why I'm calling. I've not been doin' very well, Sally."

"Oh, no, Ronny, what is it? What's wrong?"

"I can't eat, sleep or concentrate on work. I'll tell ya, Sally, I'm in a terrible way."

"What does the doctor say, Ronny?"

"Hmm, let me see, I've got his prescription here somewhere. Yes, here it is, I've been prescribed a two-day dose of Buttercup; yep, that's what it says, all right. Apparently, according to Doc anyway, that oughta fix me right up. Honest."

"Buttercup? Oh, you," Sally giggled, "Ronny, you haven't called me that in a long time."

"Haven't seen ya in a long time, and I've been missin' ya something fierce, Sally. Thought I'd drive over this coming Friday and spend the weekend. I wanna see how things are going for you in Danport. Reckon I could crash on your couch?"

"Sure! Ronny, ya know Saturday's my busiest day here at the café. I just thought maybe I should prepare you for that."

"Not a problem. I'm man enough to wear an apron and help out. In fact, I think I'll look rather fetching in one, particularly if it is pink and has ruffles."

Sally laughed. "I'll see ya this weekend then. Looking forward to it. I really am Ronny. It's been a long time. Too long. Oh, my, I gotta go. See ya soon." She hung up the phone, smiling, and rushed to pick up the food Cook had waiting for the folks sitting at the corner table.

Chapter Forty-One

SURVIVING THE NIGHT

"It ain't as bad as you think. It will look better in the morning."

-Colin Powell

It was Wednesday night, and the usual groups were meeting about town. Under the bridge, Linda lit up and took a long drag before passing off the spliff to Willie next to her. Sitting just across from her, Susie and Jarod were in a deep conversation about something or other going on between Brother Fredrick and Margret. Had Brother *I love Jesus* really been spending the night at Margaret's home? Whatever, she could care less, didn't care, and laid her head back against the tree root, enjoying the buzz of pleasure she already felt. Overhead, hanging bat-like from the bridge's underbelly, Dade watched the group, pleased with his progress.

In town, Ruth opened the door to the last of their small group, Amil, and welcomed him inside. He walked across her living room and sat next to Matthew and Alice. As Ruth took her seat next to her husband, Henry opened his Bible and said, "Pastor asked us to study this evening out of Romans, chapter 12, verse 2. As you find that passage in your

Bibles, does anyone have a need? Something we can pray about for you?"

In the basement of Community Church, Brother Fredrick had just arrived. He was grateful to Stephen who set things up for him each week so he could stop into Henry's small group meeting for a few minutes before coming here. He visited with Jessie at the refreshment table as the other youth played GaGa Ball. He had to admit, he'd been surprised to see Jessie tonight, but very pleased. God was hearing his prayers, it seemed.

Just then, Stephen walked back into the basement with the new kid from New York City. He'd wondered where Stephen had run off to after setting up the chairs for tonight's meeting. Brother Fredrick said to Jessie, "Excuse me," and walked over to greet Stephen's guest, Blake. "Hey, you two. Glad you could make it this evening. Parched? Need a pop, some chips, or cookies? Margaret made some chocolate chip cookies that are amazing. They're sitting at the end of the refreshment table next to the brownies."

Under the bridge, Willie took one last long toke and passed off to Linda, announcing he was done with weed for the night. She took a hit while watching Willie pop a handful of random pills into his mouth. Cheeks bulging, dribbling different colored tablets and capsules from his lips, with garbled words, Willie hollered, "Skittle Party!"

Thinking Willie a nut, Linda closed her eyes and chilled.

Twenty minutes later without warning, Willie abruptly slammed the back of his head against the dirt, his eyes rolled back into his head, and he began seizing. The spectacle was so shocking it yanked Linda out of her blissful respite, and she tumbled over to try and help as Jarod and Susie rushed over to Willie's contorting body. Willie's skin was cold and clammy as he began to throw up, which even in her foggy brain, Linda thought was maybe a good thing. She wasn't sure what should be done but turned his head to the side so he at least wouldn't choke on his puke. So gross. She noticed Jarod had run up to the highway where there was better reception and was hurriedly making a phone call. Oh, no, what was Jarod thinking? Was he really calling someone for help? They would all be discovered out here under the bridge. Sirens and flashing lights were headed their way moments later. She was in big trouble now. Linda almost laughed aloud when it occurred to her: in trouble with whom? Her mom was dead, and her dad was probably dead-drunk as usual. Really, he just as well be dead too, like her mom, and her brother had his head in the clouds all the time, lovin' on Jesus. Nobody cared what she did. It's funny what crosses your mind at traumatic times like this one next to her. With that thought, she exhaled fully and watched the paramedics carry Willie away up the embankment and into the ambulance. Bye-bye, Willie boy. So sad, too bad. Where was the rest of that joint?

Pastor Scott banged on Henry and Ruth's door. Ruth opened it and said, "Why, Pastor, what a nice..."

Holding his hand up, Pastor Scott said, "Sorry, Ruth, but there's an emergency. I'm here to pick up Matthew."

This was no sooner out of Pastor Scott's mouth than Matthew was standing behind Ruth putting on his coat. "What is it, Pastor? What's happened?"

"It's Willie, Matthew. It looks like he may have overdosed. He's in the emergency room." With that the two men rushed to the pastor's car and sped off into the night in the direction of the hospital.

Ruth closed the door. With concern written all over her face, she turned to face Henry, who said, "Let's pray, guys," and the group immediately bowed their heads and began to pray for Willie and Matthew, his older brother.

All but one bowed in prayer. Amil, instead, turned his gaze expectantly out the window. Looking beyond the front lawn, he spotted Dade. With a smirk on his face, Dade winked at Amil. Drugs were one of Dade's favorite tools.

Lauren went to bed feeling relieved. She'd be safe tonight. Her mother and father were together, their door was closed, and she'd heard them laughing earlier. She turned over in her bed to face the window, her focal point. The moon was full tonight. She always looked out the window, setting her focus out there on the moon, whenever he came into her room. It helped to imagine that she wasn't in the bed with him, he wasn't there with her and what was happening wasn't happening. Somehow, staring at the moon helped her be somewhere else. Anywhere else. Exhaling, thankful for a night alone without him, she began thinking about tomorrow. She'd been surprised when Mom and Dad had agreed that she could walk over to Jeannie's house after school tomorrow. How and why Dad was allowing her out of his sight and control like that, was a complete mystery to her. Maybe he'd just been put on the spot, or he and Mom were in a happy place at the moment. Who knew?

Just then her bedroom door creaked open. Surprised, Lauren's heart stopped; her mouth went dry. Dread filled her from the top of her head to the tip of her toes. Her back turned to her nemesis, she stared, concentrating hard, focusing, hypnotically wide eyed, at the full moon framed by her bedroom window. It was him. Padding up to her bedside. In a weirdly tender gesture, he leaned down to tuck her in. She could smell his smell, and it caused bile to rise up in her throat. She tried to still her breathing, closed her eyes, and pretended to be asleep as he leaned close to her ear, so close she could feel the warmth of his breath. With a deep, throaty voice he whispered, "Tell Jeannie, tell anyone about us and I'll destroy you. I'll crush you into a fine powder. Understand?"

Frozen, Lauren nodded silently but continued to face away from him. Full of self-loathing and a feeling of worthlessness, she waited until he was gone and the door to her parent's bedroom had opened and closed back, before crawling out of her bed. Numb, she stumbled into the bathroom. Locking the door behind her, she got out the razor blade she kept hidden behind the medicine cabinet and sat on the floor with her arm over the bathtub. She began to cut, raising blood drops on her skin. She watched the pain drain and leave her body. Finally, a flat calm invaded. Then euphoria. She was back in control.

Chapter Forty-Two

WITH A LITTLE HELP FROM FRIENDS

"If your friends are there, then everything's alright."
-Elton John

After school the next day, Lauren and Jeannie walked together to Jeannie's home. Jeannie thought about their plans for the afternoon to study and just hang out. To tell the truth, Jeannie had been glad her mother had encouraged her to ask Lauren again, if she could come over. She admitted to herself that at first, she could hardly stand to be around Lauren, but lately, as she'd been praying for her, she'd been filled with an empathy for her that was hard to explain. She felt Lauren's pain although she wasn't exactly sure what was causing it, so she was thankful Lauren had finally been allowed to come over. As they walked, she noticed, not for the first time, the layers of bulky clothing and long sleeves Lauren always wore. Gosh, she had to be about to burn up in all that garb, "Hey, Lauren, aren't you hot in all those layers?"

"No, I'm okay," Lauren muttered in a soft tone.
"Well, alright, but if you want to shed some of that once we get to my house, feel free. I'm getting hot just looking at ya," Jeannie laughed.

Finally, they walked up to the Pierce home, and Jeannie led the way into the kitchen through the side door. There, Lauren and Jeannie came face to face with Ruth's behind as she was bent over, pulling a large pan of brownies out of the oven. Jeannie piped loudly, "Well, hellllloooooo, Mama," and giggled at her own humor, followed by, "Gosh, Mom, those smells so good." With that, Jeannie dropped her books on the cabinet top, went over to the fridge, and pulled out a gallon of milk. "Lauren, you want a glass of milk?"

"Thank you, that'd be nice," Lauren looked up at Jeannie from her cowed down countenance.

"Lauren, we're awfully glad you got to come over today. I hope you like brownies," Ruth said as she set the hot pan of rich chocolate onto a cooling rack next to the oven.

"I do, yes, ma'am," Lauren mumbled as her eyes darted back and forth, "Smells really good."

"Mom makes the best," remarked Jeannie as she set two tall glasses of ice-cold milk on the table where Lauren was sitting.

Once the brownies had cooled enough to allow cutting without pulling and sticking to the knife, Ruth sliced two hefty pieces and set them in front of the girls, "There you go, girls. I'll leave you two to it. I've got towels to fold." Ruth headed to the utility room.

Jeannie took a giant bite and with her mouth full of chewy decadence asked, "So what do you like to do for fun, Lauren?"

Tentatively tearing her brownie into smaller chunks, Lauren muttered, "I sleep a lot."

"Oh. So, you don't play sports, sing, read or anything like that?"

"No."

"I see. Would you like to go on a walk after we finish these and get a little fresh air? Mother is always saying that fresh air and sunshine are good for the soul." Jeannie rolled her eyes. "She's really hung up on all that outdoors stuff."

"Sure."

Heather heard her mailbox open and close by the front door and glanced through the window just in time to see the mailman walking away on his way to the next house, busy delivering the mail. Hoisting herself up from the couch where she'd been reading, she waddled out onto her front porch and pulled the mail out of the mailbox attached to the brick wall by their front door. Thumbing through the envelopes, she swayed back into their living room, tossed their mail onto the coffee table in front of the couch, which had become her afternoon happy place, and went on into the kitchen to fix a tall glass of iced lemonade. She'd always loved tart lemonade. Glass in hand, she doddered her pregnant self back into the living room and collapsed onto the couch, causing the springs to squeal in protest. Feeling humongous, she rolled her eyes. Reaching for the mail, she leaned over her giant stomach, amazed by how her girth hindered bending and flexibility in general, she stretched for the pile of mail, opened the first envelope on top, the one with no return address, and began reading its contents. Tears welled up in her eyes as its words assaulted her. Who would say such horrible things? Monstrous! Such vile words! Grieved, she quickly picked up the envelope, turned it over, and looked for a name or return address. Nothing. Scott would be home any minute. Panicked because she didn't want Scott to see this letter, knowing how much it would hurt him, and for some reason unable to bring herself to destroy it, she got back up onto her swollen feet and hid the letter in her nightgown drawer.

    Brother Fredrick, Margaret, and Ben climbed out of Fred's car parked at the hospital. Walking up to the receptionist, Brother Fredrick asked what room Willie was in. Pushing the elevator button, they rode to the second floor and got off, looking for room 214. As they walked through the hospital room's doorway, they saw Matthew sitting by Willie's hospital bed. Matthew's chin was scruffy with a day-old beard, and it was obvious he'd slept in the clothes he was wearing, probably in that chair by his brother's bed, or tried to sleep. Rising, Matthew shook Brother Fredrick's hand, Margaret's, and young Ben's. "Thanks for coming by you guys. Means a lot."

"Of course," said Brother Fredrick, "How's the patient?"

"He's out of danger, thank God, but hasn't opened his eyes yet."

Margaret added, "And how are you, Matthew?"

"Doin' all right, I suppose. Willie gave us a pretty good scare. It's been touch and go. We nearly lost him."

Just then, Alice walked in with a couple of steaming coffees. "Oh, gosh, how good of you guys to stop by," she said, setting the styrofoam cups aside and hugging each one. Paying particular attention to little Ben, she bent down to his level, "and especially you, young man," she said, fist bumping his shoulder.

Ben grinned shyly, basking in the special recognition.

"Margaret, would you and Ben like to walk with me down to the children's playground? The hospital really has a nice jungle gym set up for kids. I think Ben would really enjoy it."

"Sure. Ben, does that sound like a good idea to you?"

Ben nodded enthusiastically, and the three of them left the two men alone with the patient and the coffee. Matthew offered Brother Fredrick one of the coffees and pulled out a chair for him. As the two men sat together blowing on their coffees to cool them off, they talked about nothing in particular, but Matthew noticed how the tension that had been forming in his forehead and neck began to fall away and lessen. Feeling regenerated, Matthew thought of that passage he'd read just the other day in Proverbs: *Sweet friendships refresh the soul and awaken our hearts with joy, for good friends are like the anointing oil that yields the fragrant incense of God's presence.* Amazing, but he actually was feeling stronger, refreshed, and was glad for the friendship he shared with Fred.

Meanwhile, at the hospital's playground, Alice and Margaret talked as they sat on a little bench in the play area watching Ben climb and slide with two other children. Thinking how Ben never seemed to meet a stranger, Margret asked, "What does the doctor say, Alice?"

"Doc Howard said it was close. It was really close, Margaret. Willie makes me so mad. He almost died. How stupid can a person be to cram a mouthful of who knows what into his mouth and swallow? Crazy kid," Alice said. "He's lucky to be here, Marge. Foolish, foolish boy." Tears welled up in her eyes as she shook her head in the way people do when speaking of someone, they love who's done something really stupid.

Margaret reached over and squeezed Alice's hand. "But you didn't lose him, he's still here, and we know luck had nothing to do with it."

"Yes. Thank God. Literally, thank God, Margaret. Willie is a miracle. I just hope he's not an idiot and realizes it."

Ben rushed up, "Mama, Mama, watch this. Are you watching?" he shouted over his shoulder as he ran back to the slide and began climbing the ladder.

"I'm watching, shug," Margaret hollered back.

Watching Ben, Alice said, "They start out so innocent and young, don't they? Then, I'm not sure what happens."

"Willie's gonna be fine. He'll find his way, Alice; he'll get his footing. He's got a good heart."

"I hope you're right," Alice said as a giant tear drop fell to her lap.

Margaret put her arm around Alice's shoulders and gave her a squeeze in an effort to comfort her. "Changing the subject, how long have you and Matthew dated, Alice?"

"Since grade school. I mean, if we could've dated in grade school. Actually, we've never *dated*, we've just done life together. Matthew's always been the one for me, and so I've just grown up being a part of his family. It's just been the three of us. My parents have long been out of the picture, Matthew's too, so he pretty much raised Willie on his own, and I've tried to help anywhere I could. Willie's been like a little brother to me. I watched him grow up, ya know?"

"I know friend, I know," Margret patted her friend's knee.

Holding a handful of zinnias he'd personally picked from his mother's garden, Jessie knocked on Janie's door. Opening it, she leaned against it, holding the doorknob and said, "What?"

"Peace offering," Jessie said, thrusting the flowers toward her.

"Thank you," then after an uncertain pause, "Wanna come in?"

"Yeah, that'd be great."

"Besides, you need to get your chess set out of my way," Janie quipped.

"Yeah, that's right."

"You're a D.P. man, right?"

"Right."

Janie led the way into the kitchen and began to put ice in glasses. Glancing over at the breakfast table, she said, "There's your chess set."

"Thanks."

"I guess you can sit down."

Jessie pulled out one of the chairs around the table and took a seat, setting his glass of fizzing Dr. Pepper on the table in front of him.

Janie started rummaging around under the kitchen sink and finally produced a vase, which she filled with water, then she began to expertly trim and arrange the flowers.

"Looks like you know what you're doing," said Jessie.

"I used to work in a flower shop, town before this one," she added as if an explanation were needed.

"Why'd ya'll move to Danport?"

"Too many bills came due where we were, so it was time to move on."

Embarrassed, Jessie ducked his head and said softly, "Oh."

"Yeah, it's awkward, but that's the way the lady I call *Mother* rolls."

Jessie suddenly blurted out, "Say, wanna catch a movie with me Saturday night?"

"Whoa, that was a drastic change of topic."

Jessie grinned and looked down at his lap, "Yeah, I guess that did come out kind of random. Took me a little while to work up my courage. Look, Janie, I may have lived in a sterile bubble compared to you, we may be from two different worlds, but I really like you and I'm trying. I'm obviously not doing very well, I'm not very smooth, but I..."

"Sure."

"What? Oh. Great. Okay, I'll pick you up about 6:30 Saturday evening. Sound all right?"

"I'll be ready," responded Janie as she sat the vase of flowers on the breakfast table. Sitting down across from him at the table, she said, "Got time for a game of chess before you go?"

Jessie beamed and started setting up the board.

Chapter Forty-Three
FOR THIS CHILD

For this child I prayed; and the LORD hath given me my petition which I asked of Him.

1 Samuel 1:27

For some reason, Heather hadn't been able to throw away the poison letter she'd received, so she'd hidden it in her nightgown drawer, not wanting Scott to see it. She knew how it would affect him. It caused her heart to ache, imagining how deeply its words would hurt him if he were to ever see it. She decided she would try to destroy it later in some way that wouldn't draw any attention from Scott. She'd never hidden anything from him and felt uncomfortable with the way keeping this secret made her feel, but she didn't want him asking a bunch of questions and finding out about the letter. She considered burning it, but then there would be the ashes. She might tear it up into tiny pieces and flush it, but putting stationery down in the plumbing didn't seem wise. Hmmm.... she'd have to give this some thought, she decided.

She was almost finished with the nursery and just in time; she was a week past her due date. She folded the last little sock set together and tucked it into the top left-hand drawer of the dresser. Turning to the rocking chair that had been in her family for generations, she sat down and began to assess the room. Soft grays, lavenders, pinks, sage greens, and gentle blues. Peaceful colors. Peaceful, at least in here in this place. Safe. An inner sanctum. She realized soberly that she couldn't protect her child from the harshness of the world out there where people mailed foul, horrid, letters like the one she'd received; but in here in this place for a few years at least, their child would be safe, protected. Her thoughts turned to girl name, then boy names, and she began to wonder if she and Scott had made a mistake by not learning the gender of their baby. Oh, well, she supposed it was too late to worry about that now. As she stood up from the rocker, an eruption of water burst and ran down her legs, spilling onto the new nursery carpet. She understood immediately that her water had broken. Hurrying to the phone, she called to let Scott know, and then, ever practical, she found some towels in hopes of saving the nursery's new carpet. It was finally time, she mused, as she positioned herself on the floor on all fours and began pressing to soak the water into the towels.

Inside their garage, chuckling quietly to himself, Dade cut the brake line of the Barlowe car.

Walking Snooky, Sister Jewell was just passing Pastor Scott's home when she saw him fly up the porch steps and through his front door.

"Heather, Heather? Oh, dear Lord, Heather, what are you doing down on the floor?"

"Trying to rescue our new carpet," Heather gasped as a contraction overtook her.

Tottering up just behind Pastor Scott, in the doorway of the nursery, Sister Jewell said, "Heather, I'll finish here. That carpet will be good as new by the time I'm through with it. Here let me help you up off that floor. You two get to the hospital. Now get a move on."

Scott guided Heather out the door of the nursery, grabbed her go-bag by the door and hustled her out to the garage and into their car. Putting his key into the ignition, he began to back out of the garage.

Inside their house while cleaning the nursery's carpet, Sister Jewell began to pray for Heather and the baby the young wife would soon deliver. As she prayed, she felt a nagging. Something was amiss. She couldn't quite put her finger on it, but she thought she better call for help. "Henry? It's Sister Jewell…."

Hanging up from Sister Jewell's phone call, Henry drove in what he hoped was the direction Pastor and Heather would take to get to the hospital. As he drove, he searched carefully down each street he passed and each alley. Looking high and low for Pastor's car. He really didn't know what to expect, but he'd learned a long time ago not to question Sister Jewell's naggings. If she sensed something was amiss, to use her word, then very likely, something was amiss.

Just ahead, a wreck. Henry felt his stomach lurch as he recognized Pastor Scott's car. Sickened, Henry quickly pulled over and ran to his pastor's smoking car. Thank God, Pastor Scott seemed to be fine, wriggling free, climbing out of his window, and rushing around to the passenger side door when Henry ran up next to him. Henry could hear Pastor Scott praying as he tried to pry Heather's door open. Together they were at last able to wrench it open. Taking off his coat and carefully laying it on the grass, Henry, and Scott gently laid Heather down under a nearby tree as another contraction ripped through her body.

"I don't know what happened," sobbed Pastor Scott, "I just had the car serviced so it'd be in good shape for this day, but all of the sudden the brakes wouldn't work. Are the people in the other car all right?"

The other car? For the first time, it dawned on Henry that there was another vehicle involved, and he raced off to see if he could help them just as Sheriff McGowan and a younger man pulled up. As the Sheriff and Henry helped the people in the other car, the young man who'd been in the car with the Sheriff ran over to Scott carrying a medical bag. "I have EMT training; may I help?" Ronny McGowan said to Pastor Scott as he looked down at Heather.

"Thank God you're here; yes, my wife is in labor."

The ambulance siren could be heard rounding the corner just as Channah Roni Barlowe introduced herself to the world with a robust wail.

"Thank You, Jesus," uttered Pastor Scott as he gazed down at the squirming baby girl Ronny had just handed him.

"Amen to that," followed Ronny as he clamped and cut the umbilical cord.

Once he got Heather and their new little one all settled in at the hospital, Pastor Scott ran to their house to pick up a few things for Heather she'd forgotten to put in her go-bag. He went to their chest of drawers and opened the second one down to get her a fresh nightgown so she wouldn't have to sleep in the hospital gown she was now wearing.

What's this? He pulled out the envelope addressed to them, but with no return address, tucked under Heather's gowns. Opening the envelope, he began to read the scathing words inside. He felt his face get hot, flush with rage, and imagined how the words must have hurt his sweet Heather when she'd read them. He knew his wife well enough to know that she'd probably hidden the horrid letter from him because she'd known how it would make him feel, but to keep the darned thing at all, this filth in their home, he couldn't fathom why. Why would someone write these things? How could anyone be this cruel?

Chapter Forty-Four

STEPS OF A GOOD MAN

The steps of a good man are ordered by the Lord: And he delighteth in his way.

Psalm 37:23

Ronny called earlier to deliver the big news to Sally that he was in town and had just delivered a baby. He'd absolutely been on the biggest adrenaline high of his life. He was so excited she could hardly understand what he was saying. She smiled to herself as she thought of him. She'd known Ronny as long as she could remember. He was tall, had dark hair, a bronze complexion, square jawline, black eyes and was good looking except for his crooked nose, which, for Sally, only added to his extreme attractiveness. Ronny had been on the high school wrestling team and had been really good, but it was a common back-alley fist fight that had permanently realigned his profile. They'd been juniors in high school when Jimmy had popped Ronny's nose but good. She'd heard it crack, and then it had bled like a faucet. She wondered to herself what that dumb fight had even been about in the first place.

It was so like Ronny to arrive in Danport just in time to deliver a baby. She had to laugh at the absurdity of it all, but it did seem that God really did ordain Ronny's steps. He was continually at just the right place at the right time to offer his expert assistance. He was always just in the nick of time to save the day. He was a genuine *Good Samaritan*. It would be nice having him around this weekend. She'd been so absorbed in trying to make her café a success, she'd not realized how much she'd been missing him.

In the front booth by the window sat Amil and Richard Langley in deep conversation. Amil had coyly shared all of the information he'd learned about Sally, her background and why she'd moved to Danport. Richard gobbled it up like dessert. It had been particularly delicious for Richard to learn about Sally's dad while sitting right in Sally's Café. It provided the same sort rush an exhibitionist must get. Daring. Next order of business for Amil was to turn the conversation to Henry and the church funds, which he did expertly. He'd already planted these seeds--he just needed to water and nurture them a bit. "I'm still struggling with feeling confident that my money is going into good soil, Brother Richard."

"I've been giving that some consideration, young man, and have decided that an audit is definitely in order. There's got to be accountability," said Richard.

"I'm sure you know best. I'd certainly feel more comfortable if the matter was addressed. It is hard enough to hear and understand what the pastor is talking about without adding to that, the distraction of worrying about where one's tithe is going."

"Yes, yes, that makes sense. On another note, Amil, what do you know about that youth from New York City?"

"Blake Williams?"

"I believe so, yes, that's his name. Strange lad, I must say," Richard cocked his head.

"I've seen him hanging out with some of the church youth lately, Stephen in particular."

"I see. Stephen has no supervision or guidance at home; perhaps I should say something to him. I'd hate to see his reputation tarnished by the influence of that fop."

"Why, Brother Langley!"

Ignoring Amil's surprise, Richard got up from the table. "Excuse me, Amil," and walked abruptly out the door of Sally's little Café toward Amil's employer, Sister Joselyn, who'd suddenly drawn his attention out on the sidewalk.

Stuck with the tab, Amil paid for their coffee, noticing Richard was now in a deep conversation just outside the café, with Sister Joselyn. Richard seemed to be giving her the low down. Perfect.

After her conversation with Richard outside Sally's Café, Sister Joselyn feverishly raced home, another poison letter churning in her gut, ready to be regurgitated onto paper. Taking pen in hand, she began her next masterpiece. She adored the way this pen flowed. Only a writer would appreciate the importance of a good pen. This was a good pen. The kind of pen worthy of the task at hand. This letter was going to be the best she'd written so far. Her mouth literally watered in anticipation as she began to write. *You think you're so clever. We know your secret, Sally-dally. Did you really think we wouldn't find out that you are the daughter of a murderer? A prisoner? You thought you could run away from it. Escape it. You thought your past wouldn't catch up with you. Well, it has. We know. We know everything. You're a low life. A bad seed. The fruit doesn't fall far from the tree, ya know.* She addressed the envelope to Sally Morgan, formally of Riverside, she chuckled to herself. Placing the stamp carefully in the right-hand corner, she sealed it with her plentiful saliva.

The nurse rolled a wheelchair into Willie's hospital room. He was finally going to be released. "Hey, I don't need a wheelchair."

"Hospital rules young man. You have to ride out of here," said the nurse.

Matthew hoisted up Willie's few belongings, tossing them in a bag with the hospital freebies, that weren't really free. They all cost a fortune. Alice grabbed the book Matthew had been reading and the half bag of dry roasted peanuts he'd snacked on.

Just as they were about to roll out, Pastor Scott stepped into the room, "Hey, Willie, I wanted to see you again before you left. Feels pretty great to be going home, I'm sure."

"Yeah, I can hardly wait to be in my own bed, ya know?"

"I do know; yes, I know that feeling very well," said Pastor Scott rubbing his lower back, "Willie, I want to encourage you to join our youth group on Wednesday night. Maybe start hanging out some with Brother Fredrick and his group of kids instead of under the bridge."

Flushing with shame, understanding that his pastor apparently knew all about the bridge parties they held every Wednesday evening, Willie responded, "Yeah, that'd probably be a pretty good idea."

Matthew patted his little brother on the shoulder and then looked into the eyes of his pastor. How's that beautiful little girl of yours, Channah, is that right?"

"Oh, man, I'm telling you, she's totally amazing! I've got about a million pictures," Pastor Scott chuckled.

Matthew smiled broadly. "Hope to see every single one of them real soon, Pastor."

Alice asked, "How's Heather?"

"She's a champ, let me tell you. She definitely showed me why women rule the world."

"What? Oh, a joke," Alice laughed.

"Well, maybe, maybe not," Pastor Scott smiled, tossing his head. "You better get this train rollin'.

Hope to see each of you guys this Sunday."

"You will Pastor, you will," said Matthew as he followed the nurse who pushed his little brother out the door of the hospital room.

Finally, home and rested, Matthew was out in his workshop early the next morning. He took the clean terry cloth and like a seasoned masseur, methodically kneaded and buffed the Odie's oil into the beautiful walnut, bringing out its rich waves of dark grain. He was pleased with the look of the purple heart he'd inlaid into its surface. As he admired God's full-bodied workmanship beneath his fingertips, Matthew thought about yesterday when he and Alice brought Willie home from the hospital. What a relief it had been to see Henry sitting on their front steps, waiting for them here at the house when they pulled up into the driveway with their patient.

"Matthew, I've already fed and watered your cattle, and I'll start early in the morning, plowing that North 40; you don't need to worry about a thing 'cept getting Willie back on his feet."

"Henry, how can we ever thank you?"

"You can thank me by gobbling up that pan of cinnamon rolls Ruth baked for you before I get to 'em," Henry said patting his flat stomach. "I don't need the calories. I left a whole pan of 'em, lathered in icing that is to die for, sitting in there on your kitchen counter. Makes my mouth water just thinking about 'em, especially all that icing," said Henry rolling his eyes.

Alice looked at Willie and grinned as she helped him up the steps of the front porch, "You can count on us, Henry. We'll do our best to help you fight the fight and save you from the cinnamon rolls."

Matthew wasn't sure how people managed without the help and support of friends like Henry and Ruth, but he supposed there were some who did. He was thankful not to be one of 'em.

Ronny pulled up to Sally's little café Friday evening just as she was locking up to walk to the hospital. They'd planned on seeing the Barlowes' new baby girl tonight. Their goal was to leave the new parents undisturbed but manage to steal a little peak at Channah through the viewing window of the hospital nursery. Sally promised he'd enjoy the walk to the hospital. It was such a nice evening, and the walk would give them a chance to stretch their legs and visit, so he was glad when he arrived at her café in time go.

He'd not forgotten how beautiful Sally was, but as he gazed at her almond complexion and shapely figure, he was reminded of why he'd wanted to see this pretty brunette with the button nose and large brown saucer eyes. Stunning.

She'd told him she lived above her new enterprise, Danport's favorite café, so he figured he'd just leave his vehicle and overnight bag parked right where they sat. He and Sally could walk together from here to the hospital, he thought, as he got out of his pickup and strolled up to her.

"Hello there, stranger." Sally's smile could not hide the deep sadness in her eyes.

"Good to see ya, Buttercup," Ronny said hugging and kissing her on the cheek. "Ready?"

"Yeah, I'm all set, let's go."

As they walked, Ronny shared every detail of this afternoon's delivery of little Channah. In his excitement, he babbled on and on before finally winding down and realizing that Sally hadn't said a word. He'd not even given her a chance to say a word. Pausing he asked, "How've you been, Sally?"

"Oh, I've been alright, I..." her voice cracked, and she was unable to say more. With eyes welling up, one tear finally broke free, tumbling over and making its way down her cheek. She wasn't sure why being with Ronny was causing her to be so emotional.

"Hey, hey, come here," Ronny said as he tried to embrace her.

"No, let's keep walking. I don't want to make a big spectacle out here on the sidewalk. Remember, people here don't know anything about me. They'd wonder what my problem was if they saw me wailing out here. New topic, uh, let's see," she said wiping her eyes with both hand and sniffing loudly. "Okay, what brings you to Danport, Mr. McGowan?"

"Just following my doctor's orders. Isn't my needing to get a little Buttercup-fix more than enough reason to be here?"

Sally punched his bicep playfully and laughed. "Yeah, that's good enough for me. I'm glad you're here, Ronny McGowan. I could use a friend right now."

Chapter Forty-Five
SHARE WITH OTHERS

And do not forget to do good and to share with others, for with such sacrifices God is pleased.

Hebrews 13:16

Saturday whipped by quickly at the little café. Ronny couldn't believe how busy the place was every minute of that long day or how exhausting it was to be on one's feet all that time. After the last customer left the building and the door was locked, Ronny tried to recover as Sally boxed up the supper and pie, she planned on delivering to the Barlowes. Sally said the Pastor's home was within walking distance and a pleasant walk at that, so they were going to stroll together to deliver the meal she'd prepared; but right now, he was seriously wondering if he'd be able to take one more step. Sitting with his feet up, he could feel his legs throbbing in waves that ran clear down to his toes. *How did Sally do it day after day,* he wondered? He'd never been this tired in his life.

The hospital only kept Heather and the baby overnight. Mother and child had just been released this afternoon. Channah would be spending her first night at home.

"Hey, let me help you with some of that," Ronny hollered as he rushed up to Sally, surprised that he was able to move. Sally worked all day waiting tables and managed to prepare all this food for the Barlowes, too. She was incredible.

Sally juggled some of the hot catering boxes into Ronny's waiting arms as he asked, "Gosh, are you feeding a harvest crew? This would surely be enough to do it," he laughed.

Already feeling better, Sally responded with a smile, "No, I just wanted to make sure they had plenty. I figured they'd be having company, and what they don't eat now, they can freeze."

"Smells fabulous."

"Hope you're right."

They began the walk together down the sidewalk toward Pastor Scott's home. It was a cool fall night, but neither of them was chilly. The flush of being with each other, their arms laden with hot food and their light jackets kept them plenty warm.

"Okay, no changing the subject this time--how've you been?"

"All right, I suppose. I work long hours trying to keep the café afloat, and that way I don't have a lot of time to think about the past," Sally answered.

"Is that good, though?"

"What do you mean?"

"I don't know; just wondered if maybe the past should be dealt with," Ronny pointed out.

Sally glared at him.

Ronny freed the hand he had under the boxed pie and stuck it out defensively, "Hey, hey, hey. Sorry. I'll get back in my lane. Fast," he finished. Looking straight ahead resolutely, he tucked his hand back under the boxed pie where it belonged.

Leaning her shoulder into him affectionately, Sally admitted, "No, Ronny, it's me. I'm the one at fault. I'm the one who should be sorry. I know you care about me and just want to help. I'll tell you what. We'll talk later all you want, okay?"

Grinning, Ronny responded, "Sure thing, Buttercup," to which Sally rolled her eyes and groaned.

Stepping up onto the Pastor's front porch, they were greeted by Sister Jewell who answered the door, hugged Sally warmly and then began directing them toward the kitchen where Ruth was busy washing dishes and Jeannie was drying and stacking.

Ruth said, "Hey Sally, who've you got there?"

"Ladies, please make the acquaintance of Ronny McGowan. Ronny and I have known each other since kindergarten."

Drying her hands on her apron, Ruth shook Ronny's hand, "McGowan? Any relation to our sheriff?"

"He's my uncle."

"Well, it's a pleasure to meet you, Ronny."

"It certainly is son. I understand you delivered our little Channah yesterday morning," said Sister Jewell.

"Seriously?" squealed Jeannie, bouncing over to the group in the kitchen's center. "That's awesome."

Shyly, Ronny responded, "Just happened to be at the right place at the right time."

"It's a thing with him. It's always been that way with Ronny," Sally reminisced. "As long as I've known him, he's always been the right man, in the right place, at the right time. You might call him a *for such a time as this* kind of guy."

"Indeed. You were definitely the man for the moment yesterday morning, son, no doubt about that," said Sister Jewell. "Follow me. I think you should be properly introduced to the Barlowes."

Ronny and Sally set the food they'd brought on the kitchen countertops and followed Sister Jewell to a bedroom door where she paused and knocked, "Pastor? Heather? Is this a good time? There's someone here who'd like to meet you formally."

"Formally? Sure, Sister Jewell, come on in," said Pastor, rising to go to the door. When the door opened and he saw that it was Ronny, the EMT guy, who'd happened to show up yesterday just in time to deliver his child, his eyes welled up with tears of gratitude. "It's you," he said, clasping Ronny's hand in both of his until Ronny opened his arms and brought the pastor into an embrace.

"Yes, sir, it's me," he said, patting the pastor on the back. "Sally and I brought you some supper. Well, Sally prepared it all; I just helped to carry it here, which is probably a good thing since she's a way better cook than I am," Ronny added grinning. "How's our little girl?"

"She's perfect," Sister Jewell responded from behind Ronny and Sally.

"Sally," Pastor Scott hugged her, "Thank you for making us a meal."

"Oh, she didn't make you just one meal. You've got enough in there for several," laughed Ronny.

Channah's gurgles and squeaks were heard from over in the afternoon shadows of the room where Heather sat in a rocker. "Oh, my, that must be the most beautiful sound in the world," said Sally.

Heather asked, "Wanna hold her?"

Moving swiftly over to Heather, Sally asked, "Could I?"

Rising out of the rocker, Heather said, "Of course," as she handed little Channah to Sally.

Holding baby Channah, Sally sat down slowly into the rocker, sighing her contentment.

Ronny looked on, thinking to himself that he'd never seen a more beautiful picture.

Pastor Scott put his hand on Ronny's shoulder. "Come over here with me." As they walked closer to the newborn he said, "Ronny, I'd like you to officially meet Channah Roni Barlowe."

Ronny looked at him in disbelief, "Ronny?"

"Well, we used the feminine spelling, R-O-N-I, but yes. You were a godsend yesterday morning, Ronny. A true blessing. Channah will carry your name with her for as long as she lives. Hopefully, she will distinguish it by being the kind of blessing you were to us."

"Thank you, Pastor. I'm so honored. Would it be all right if I prayed for Channah Roni before Sally and I leave?"

"Never gonna turn that down. Let me get our kitchen help in here with us before you start. I know they'll want to be a part of it."

Soon the small bedroom was crowded as everyone gathered around the newborn, and Ronny laid his hands on her little head and prayed.

Willie had been glad to get home. It was strangely difficult to rest in a hospital. It seemed they'd awakened him all through the night to check on this and that. At last, he was home and could really get some rest. He couldn't believe he was still here. Alive. He'd thought surely that handful of who knows what kind of pills would've been the end of him. Why couldn't it have been the end of him?

There was a knock on the front door. Matthew answered, "Hello, guys, come on in," followed by voices and footsteps approaching Willie's bedroom. Willie groaned in dread. He had company.

Into Willie's room walked brother and sister, Stephen and Linda. "Hey, Willie," Stephen smiled, "looks like you're doing better than the last time I saw you in the hospital."

"Yeah, I'm feeling a lot better all right," said Willie.

"Hey, Willie," Linda greeted him sheepishly, sitting down at the foot of his bed.

"Linda," returned Willie, in a flat tone.

Laying a stack of comics on Willie's bedside table, Stephen said, "We brought you some reading material. Never too old for Marvel Comics, right, Willie?"

"Right," Willie answered, barely audible.

"Well, I'll let you kids visit. I've gotta pay bills," Matthew said as he left the room.

Stephen asked, "Is there anything else we can get for you or do for you, Willie?"

"Nah," *just leave. Leave me alone*, Willie thought to himself. "Matt takes pretty good care of me, and Alice has stocked our refrigerator full of food and casseroles. We oughta be set for quite a while, I figure."

"Willie, I was hoping you would come to youth group with me this coming Wednesday evening. I can come by and pick you up, if you'd like, so you won't have to walk into our meeting all alone. I know sometimes the first walk-in can be daunting. What do you think?"

"I don't know, Stephen. Let me think about it."

"Sure, Willie, no pressure. I'll check back with you later," said Stephen gently.

Moody, Linda sat staring at the wall as her brother stood.

"Come on, Linda, we better get home and get started on our homework," Stephen said.

Slowly getting to her feet, Linda mumbled, "Yeah."

"Check with you later, Willie," and with that Willie was alone again and relieved to be so. He could hear the adding machine clicking off numbers in the other room as Matthew paid bills. He knew his little adventure to the emergency room had set them back plenty. Tucking his head in self-loathing, he sucked in air and wondered why he couldn't get it right. Why couldn't he get his act together? He was a walking disaster.

Having delivered the meal to Pastor Scott and his new little family, Sally and Ronny walked back to the café. "Does anyone in Danport know about what happened, Sally?"

"Well, I've certainly not told anyone. I don't know, I suppose your uncle, being the sheriff and all, has probably figured it out, but he's not a gossip, so maybe my secret is safe."

"Oh, you can count on that. He's a good man. Mum is the word when it comes to Uncle Jack. So how have you been, Sally?"

"Honestly? I've been in a deep dark pit, if you wanna know the truth. Don't believe I've ever felt this low, but the constant work at the café and just trying to stay out of the red have helped me stay afloat emotionally if that makes sense?"

"I'm sure the hard work does help, but you're still grieving, Sally; of course, it makes sense that you'd be horribly depressed."

"Yes, I'm sure that's part of it. That and the gnawing suspicion that Daddy really did do it. Ronny..." Sally's voice caught. She'd never spoken that aloud to anyone before. She tried desperately to regain her composure. Sally knew she was an ugly crier. If the dam broke, there would not just be tears, but contorted lips, snot, and drool. Nevertheless, she could hold back no longer and finally burst with sobs as a wet flood tumbled down her cheeks, "Ronny, I think my dad really did kill my mom!"

"What? No, no, I don't think so, Sally."

Sally squinted at him through the blur of salty liquid filling her eyes. "What do you know, Ronny? Why would you say that? He was convicted. He's in prison now." Why would you think he didn't do it?"

"My gut. I always trust my gut, Sally," he said as he took her in his arms, shushing her crying. "You just can't know for sure that he did it, Sally-girl."

Between hiccups and sobs, Sally argued, "But a jury found him guilty, Ronny."

"Yes, but I've been doing some digging. That's one of the reasons I'm here. I want to talk a few things over with you. I sincerely think your dad may be innocent."

Finally arriving at their destination, Sally put her key in the café door while Ronny got some hanging clothes out of his pickup for church tomorrow. Walking up behind Sally, she flipped on the lights of the cafe, and they walked in together. "I really like your place, Sally. You've been working me so hard since I got here, I'd not had a chance to tell you."

She punched him in the arm. "Oh, you," she smiled and turned to put on a kettle of water. "Tea?"

"Yeah, that sounds good."

There was a comfortable silence between them for several minutes before Sally said, "Thanks, Ronny."

"For what?"

"For everything. For being here, for believing in my dad, and for just listening to me. For just being you."

Ronny laid his church clothes over a chair in the center of the empty café and slid into a booth. "Well, I had to come, Sally. Doctor's orders."

Sally laughed as she brought over two hot cups of tea and sat across from him in the booth. "So, what have you dug up about Daddy?"

Chapter Forty-Six

SONS

Even a child is known by his doings, whether his work be pure, and whether it be right.

Proverbs 20:11

Entering their dark home, Stephen and Linda were instantly assaulted by the strong stink of body grease, urine, and vomit. Looking directly into his eyes, Linda said, "I'm going out," and turned to leave.

Hollering after her, Stephen tried to get her to stop, but she was gone. Turning his attention away from her and to the figure sitting slumped in the shadows on the couch, Stephen crouched down next to his stubble-faced father and said, "Dad, come on. Let's get you up and into the shower."

A compliant drunk, Stephen's father tried to help. Struggling to his feet, he began to cry. "I'm sorry, Son. I'm so sorry," he slurred.

The stench of his father wafted over Stephen as he caught a glimpse through the living room window of Linda's headlights pulling away from the house and speeding off into the night. Feeling as though he was losing the battle, he shouldered the weight of his father, guiding him to the bathroom. Setting him down on the closed toilet seat, Stephen started the water in the shower. First testing it to make sure it wasn't too hot, he then began to help his father undress, talking to him in a soft soothing voice, saying words he wasn't sure he himself even believed. "It's gonna be all right, Dad. We're gonna get through this. You'll see."

"I miss her, Stevie. I can't go on without her. I remember the night she died..." and with that Stephen's father began to recite, down to the most minute detail, the events of the night his mother had passed away. Not only had he himself been there and lived it, but Stephen had also heard his dad tell it, the same story, a million times. In fact, almost every time he and his father had a conversation, this was the script.

His dad refused to clean out her closet, allow anyone to move her shoes from the last place she left them, or put up the book, which remained open to the page she was last reading, her glasses sitting on top, both on the end table beside her chair. Her toothbrush was still in its stand there by the sink, her perfume and jewelry on the tray of her dressing table, and he still kept the pantry stocked with her favorite cookie.

Full of compassion, Stephen couldn't bring himself to force his father to pack up her things until he was ready. The problem was Stephen was beginning to wonder if his dad would ever be ready. "Here, Dad, sit on this seat in the shower and let the water hit your chest while I scrub your back. Maybe a righteous back scrubbin' will feel good and help you relax," Stephen said as he began rubbing the bar of soap back and forth on the wet bristles of the scrub brush to make up a lather.

"There was the terrible diagnosis, then it metastasized, she was gasping for air. Son, I did everything I could to help her, I promise I did, but I just couldn't save her."

"Of course you did everything you could, Dad; no one doubts you did your very best to save Mom. It was just her time to go. Hold still while I shampoo your hair. Hey, after I get your hair rinsed, why don't you let me run a razor over that mug of yours? Might be a good idea while we're at it, don't you think?"

"She's gone, Stevie. Gone," Stephen's dad cried.

"It'll be all right, Dad. We're gonna be Okay. Mom would want us to try. She'd want us to live for her. She'd want us to make her proud," Stephen said using the rosewood shaving brush to suds up his father's face. He liked the sandalwood fragrance of the beard soap he'd picked up yesterday. He held his dad's razor under hot water. "We're gonna try our best to make Mom proud, right, Dad? Okay?"

"Sure son, sure."

Just as Stephen was positioning himself to take the first swipe at his dad's whiskers with the razor, he heard knocking at the front door. "I'll be right back, Dad. You all right to sit here for a spell?"

His dad nodded, then hung his head allowing the water to beat down and wash all the just applied beard soap off his face. Upon seeing this, Stephen sighed and then walked out of the steamy bathroom. Opening the front door, Stephen saw Sister Jewell standing under the porch light with an armful of dinner. It was steaming hot and countered his father's body odor in the affirmative, "Hey, Sister Jewell."

"Good evening, young man," Sister Jewell said, noticing Stephen's wet shirt sleeves. "I thought you all could use a little tender lovin' care about right now." Her nose wrinkled up as she looked passed him and nodded. "I can see I was right," and with that she barged right in, walking straight for the kitchen. "I'll put this in the oven to keep it warm until you're ready," she said, closing the oven door on the meal she'd brought. Without asking permission or if her intrusion was even wanted, she left the kitchen and charged into the utility room, found the hamper and began to separate laundry.

"Oh, ma'am, you don't have to do that, honest. I was gonna get to it as soon as I could. I'd be embarrassed for you to see my underwear and stuff."

"Boy, do you think I've lived this long and haven't seen a man's undergarments? Now you go do whatever you were doing while I tidy this place up."

Unable to come up with a rebuttal, Stephen surrendered and ambled back into the bathroom to finish shaving his dad.

When Stephen and his father finally emerged from the bathroom, Dad looked like a new man, squeaky clean and in fresh clothes, wrinkled though they be. Their eyes widened to see the magic Sister Jewell had worked in such a short time. They could hear the washing machine agitating and the dishwasher churning as they sat down at their dining room table, which had been perfectly set with place mats and all the trimmings. With an apron tied around her wide waist, Sister Jewell hobbled out of the kitchen, carrying the entrée and invited them to fill their plates. For the first time in a very long while, Stephen began to have hope.

Removing her apron and sitting down across from Stephen, Sister Jewell winked at him and said,

"Now then, gentlemen, I'm supposing you won't mind if I bless this food?"

Stephen smiled with gratitude in Sister Jewell's direction as they joined hands around the table, and she began to pray.

When Jessie asked his dad if he could borrow the lawn mower, edger and pickup, his dad looked at him whimsically and questioned, "All right. I give, what's up? You feeling feverish? Here, let me check for a temperature," he said, reaching Jessie's forehead. Are you telling me that you are voluntarily wanting to do yard work?"

When Jessie explained the plan to his father, who readily agreed that it was a very good plan, his dad still couldn't resist a little dig at his son. "It's amazing what a guy will do to win the favor of a beautiful girl, isn't it?" With a shake of his head, Jessie's dad laughed heartily, enjoying his own humor immensely.

Permission granted, tools obtained, Jessie struck out in the direction of the Robertson's home. If he hurried, he could finish before Janie got home from auditions. She was in vocal music, and they were having tryouts today after school for next year's jazz choir. He knew she'd do great. He'd once heard her sing and had been very impressed.

Pulling up to Janie's home, he got out of the pickup, hauled the lawn mower out of the bed, cranked it up and began mowing.

Brother Fredrick and Ben pulled up to Ben's home. "How were your burger and fries, Ben?"

"So good. I'm as full as a fat little tick," Ben patted his pushed-out tummy as he ogled the man he'd grown to admire.

Brother Fredrick chuckled at the little man in the passenger seat of his car. "A fat little tick, huh?"

"Yep."

Glancing at Ben's empty driveway, he said, "Looks like your mama isn't home yet. She said she might have to work late this evening. I think they've got a big child custody case tomorrow. Dr. Mulligan is scheduled to testify, so they'll be in court for much of the morning. Why don't we go on inside and start on your homework."

Ben grinned affirmation at Brother Fredrick, and they started up the sidewalk. Once on the porch, Brother Fredrick removed his key to Margaret's front door and opened it.

Peering through her living room curtains from across the street, ever the busy body, Sister Joslyn looked on, aghast. *He actually has his own key! Decency is apparently too archaic for today's dating scene*, she thought, buzzing with a huff as she shoved the curtain back in place with revulsion and stormed toward the back of her house and outside to her garden where Amil was working. "Amil, you absolutely won't believe the latest...."

Amil smiled to himself, certain that he probably knew exactly what her version of *the latest* would be. Bound to Dade, he'd risen to liege lord influencer, a virtuoso of subterfuge, orchestrating countless similar calamities in church after church across the country. He was a wizard at manipulation.

"How they fall, how they fall. Brother Fredrick *was* such a good man, Amil, until he fell under the spell of that hussy. She has corrupted him!

Oh, my dear, I tell you, she has corrupted him. It's despicable what she's done to his once fine reputation," Sister Joslyn raved.

Adept at his sport, Amil added fuel to the fire. "Have you discussed the situation with Widow Camilla? Or Captain Parker?"

"I'll see them this evening for bridge. It has become such a delicate matter, of utmost importance, it should definitely be handled by the pillars of our church fellowship, people with experience and seasoning. Especially since Pastor Scott," she spat disapprovingly, "refuses to grasp that this is a crisis of the highest form. It could tarnish our entire church."

Planting his words carefully in this fertile soil, Amil cunningly leaned in. "Of course, but Pastor Scott is young. His sermons are, well, I wouldn't call them meaty. I'm sure with a little maturity his sermons will begin to make more sense. He just doesn't have the wisdom or life experience that you do, ma'am, that the old guard has. Yes, you must protect the church at all costs. If not you, then who? Have you sought the counsel of Roda and George Brackens?"

"No. Excellent idea, Amil, I'll call immediately and see if they're also free this evening."

An unscrupulous master enchanter, Amil twisted the knife in up to the hilt, cultivating the seeds he'd sown with the ease of a pro. "What about Wanda and Frank?"

"Oh, Amil, I could just kiss you."

Amil feigned the blush of humble innocence. Oh, he was good.

"Of course, they need to be made aware--" Sister Joselyn animated, "they should definitely be there this evening, too. Yes, I'll go make the calls right now," she gasped breathlessly as she buzzed back effervescently into her kitchen and straight to her phone.

Once Sister Joslyn was out of earshot, Dade handed Amil the new hose he'd just screwed into the hydrant. Amil's face hardened as he grabbed it. Ripping the hose from Dade's grip, he glared at his ever-present daemon. Try as he may, he could not escape his tormentor. Dade spit into the rich soil Amil had just turned over, and smoke rose from the wet spot his spittle left in the earth. Imperious, Dade crossed his arms and leaned against the hot brick of the house,

"Oh, Amil, I could just kiss you," he mimicked Sister Joslyn in a high pitch while batting his eyes.

Amil lunged at him, ready to strangle the life out of him at last, but Dade was suddenly gone, vanished, leaving only the wretched bouquet of dung, sulfur and stagnant water, the toxic potpourri that always accompanied his assailant, a noxious malodor stung Amil's nose. Furious tears welled up in Amil's eyes. He would never be free.

Chapter Forty-Seven

EXPOSED

"You never know what someone is dealing with behind closed doors. You only know what you see or what you think you see."
-Mackenzie Phillips

Jeannie and Lauren sat together under the tree in the park. They'd not quite made it to the park when they got to talking about boys and who was the cutest in trigonometry, and without much thought they sat down together on the bench as they continued their discussion. Comfortable at long last, Lauren had finally begun to relax around Jeannie and talk with her like a regular teenager, like a girlfriend. Jeannie treasured their discussions and had decided that Lauren was actually pretty fun to hang out with. Lauren hadn't been allowed to come over to Jeannie's house again, so they'd gotten into the habit of walking this far together after school each day, to this park before splitting up, each to go their own way toward their respective homes.

Lauren was looking at a daisy she'd pulled, twirling it between her thumb and finger, talking about Ralph, a boy in their class, when her father's car squealed up to the curb of the park. He looked furious. Rabid.

Lauren instantly stopped talking, the flower fell from her fingers as she looked up at him and stood stiffly. She was horrified. Jeannie felt as if she and Lauren were communicating telepathically. She could read everything on Lauren's face. Lauren had been found out. Jeannie had never guessed that something so innocent as their walking home from school together each afternoon could be a problem for Lauren, but in an instant, she knew it was. She knew that this had been Lauren's secret from her parents, and she'd just been found out.

Without saying a word to Jeannie, Lauren's eyes connected with her father's, and she walked as if hypnotized, like a fish being reeled in to his car and got into the passenger side. Jeannie sat very still on the bench, watching, as he seethed in anger at Lauren, seemingly unaware of Jeannie's attentive presence nearby. She couldn't believe the way his face was contorting in pure fury. She could hear only his muffled voice, enraged, through the closed-up car as he screamed in pantomime at her friend, who looked down at her lap mournfully.

After they pulled away from the park's curb, all Jeannie could think about was the expression on Lauren's face when her dad had screeched up in his car. After sitting for some time in disbelief, Jeannie bent to pick up the daisy Lauren had dropped, rose from the park bench, and began the rest of her walk home. With each step, she prayed for Lauren. She didn't know what exactly, but something was very wrong in Lauren's house, and at the center of the problem was Mr. Miller.

It was finally Saturday evening. Jessie had looked forward to this moment all week. After he got off work, he drove home to take a shower. He'd cleaned up his car during his lunch break and had ironed his shirt last night. He was ready. He didn't want to run into any obstacles. Tonight was going to be perfect. He hoped.

Stepping into his home, he hollered in no particular direction, "Hey Mom, I'm home."

"Hi, honey. How was work today?"

"Oh, the usual, ya know; the customer is always right."

"That's the attitude, my dear boy. I'm sure Mr. Winthrop appreciates your outlook," his mom complimented. "You and Janie have big plans tonight?"

"Oh, I thought we'd catch a movie. That new one with Timothy Chalamet?"

"Who?"

Laughing, Jessie bellowed back, "Oh, never mind, Mom. I'm gonna hop in the shower."

"Sounds good. Oh, by-the-way, I left a little mad money for you on your dresser. Thought you and Janie might want to get an ice cream or something. Maybe after the movie with that Sha-La-Moo guy?"

"Thanks, Mom," Jessie laughed. "Sha-La-Moo," he said to himself as he nodded his head. After showering he finished getting ready and within thirty minutes was driving in the direction of Janie's home, whistling. Pulling up to her house, he noticed Duncan's big truck parked on the Robertson's lawn and shook his head in frustration. It had just rained, so Duncan's giant pickup tires had torn major grooves in the grass. It was a mess, and after all the work Jessie had put into mowing and edging. Who would do that?

Opening her front door to him, Janie gave him the shush sign with her pointer finger, turned to grab her purse, stepped out where he stood on the front porch, quietly closing the door behind her.

Jessie asked, "Are they in there?"

"Yeah. They rolled in, literally, as you can see," she said pointing at Duncan's pickup truck in her front yard, "around 5:00 this morning. Mom was crashing and banging around in the kitchen, like a bull in a china cabinet, somewhere around 1:00 this afternoon, I presume, trying to find something for them to eat. Good luck with that. She then had a major collision with the coffee table in our living room on her return trip back to her bedroom. I did some house cleaning and dishes this afternoon but haven't seen or heard hide nor hair of either of them since Mom's earlier expedition in search of food. Thankfully."

"Wow."

"It isn't even a wow to me anymore, Jessie. It's just my life. That's why I was glad you were baptized in fire the first night we hung out together, you know the night we tried to play chess? I wanted you to know what you were getting into, so I kinda set you up, letting you come over. It was kind of a test to see if you were really interested in me, see if you'd stay the course, find out if you'd ask me out again after you knew. I figured Mom would make it home at some point while you and I were hanging out that night, so you learned the hard way. What happened that night is standard operating procedure in our little family's world. My world. My goal is to do better."

"Oh, Janie, bless your…"

"'Nuff of that. You look nice tonight, good sir. I like that shirt."

"Whoa. Talk about shutting me down and changing the subject."

"Well, ya know, when you live the subject, you sometimes lose your taste for it, for rehashing it. Nothing personal."

"None taken. Makes perfect sense to me," Jessie said stiffly, "and thank you."

Smiling at him, her voice softened as she leaned toward him, "Don't be offended, Jessie, okay? I'd wanted to be completely upfront with you, so I made sure you got an eyeful that first night you came to the house. I'm sorry, but like I said, it was kind of a test to see if you'd come back, see if you'd ever call me again after you knew the whole truth. Now you know. Nuff said. I'd just thought you should know right off the bat, everything about my mom and me. Especially, if you and I are gonna be an item."

"Wait, we're gonna be an item?"

Giggling, Janie asked, "You going to keep mowing our lawn?"

"Sure, if it helps you, Janie, sure."

"Well, thanks for that. You're a pretty great guy, Jessie," she said, scooting closer to him as he pulled away from her home. "So, what's on tonight's agenda?" She kissed him lightly on the cheek.

Blushing slightly, he cleared his throat and said, "I thought we'd see that new movie with Timothy Chalamet."

"I love him. That sounds great, Jessie," laying her head on his shoulder. "Sorry, but I'm absolutely exhausted for some reason."

As he drove, Jessie thought to himself about Janie and him being an item. He liked the sound of that. He wasn't sure how she managed, what with her mom not getting home until 5:00 this morning. He could easily imagine that Janie really was exhausted, extremely so. Who wouldn't be? In fact, she was probably worn plumb out, what with the anxiety, worry and waiting up for her mom, and not just last night, but it seemed to be every night. Night after night. It had to be taking a toll on her. Janie acted like it didn't bother her, it was just her life, she was used to it, and it was no big deal, but Jessie wasn't insensitive; he noticed that Janie had waited up for her mom last night, making sure she made it home safe and sound, even noting the time she'd finally rolled in. Janie had been up all night long, until early this morning, waiting. He smiled as he heard soft snoring coming from his date.

Jeannie did a backward dive, plopping down on her parents' bed, crushing a pillow against her stomach with her arms, "Oh, Mom, you can't even believe how horrible he was, is. It was awful. Lauren was horrified. I was horrified. There we were at the park, completely innocent. It wasn't like we were doing anything wrong, you know. He looked like a monster. How could Mr. Miller treat his daughter that way? What a brute."

Ruth continued to put clothes up in the dresser drawers. "I'm not sure, Jeannie. Something seems terribly wrong there, I've got to admit. I hope you don't mind, but I've spoken to Helen about Lauren."

"Gee, I'm not sure if Lauren would be okay with that."

"I didn't use Lauren's name, but I felt like we needed to take some sort of action, talk with a professional to find out if there really was something to what we've both been observing, and, if so, what we should do to help."

"What did she say?"

"Well, she agreed that it didn't sound like Lauren has a happy homelife, but apparently, nothing much can be done at this point unless we somehow get Lauren to talk, to fill us in on what's wrong."

"Boy, that's a tall order, Mom. There hasn't been much opportunity to build trust with her to where she'd feel like she could confide in me, you know? Mr. Miller will hardly let Lauren out of his sight. School, church, and home. Even walking home after school is apparently allotted only a certain amount of time. He keeps her on a pretty tight leash. He's a real control freak."

"I suspect that's by design. Poor Lauren. How dreadful for her."

"I'll try to call her. See if she can come over tomorrow after church." Jeannie pulled her cell phone out of the back pocket of her jeans and tapped out the Miller's landline number. "Hello, Mrs. Miller, this is Jeannie. Jeannie Pierce. Yes, ma'am, doing fine and how are you today? Good. Is Lauren there? May she talk on the phone with me for a moment?"

Suddenly, Mr. Miller's brusque voice was on the other end of the line, "Hello? Who's calling?"

Jeannie could hear Mrs. Miller sputter and whine in the background, "Johnny? Johnny?"

Startled, Jeannie forged ahead, "Mr. Miller. Good afternoon. It's Jeannie Pierce. I was wondering if Lauren could come to the phone?"

"No. Sorry. She's not available at the moment," he clipped. Abruptly, the phone line went dead.

Jeannie let out a gasp of shock as she stared at the phone. Ruth turned to face her daughter, neither sure what step to take next. Obviously, Mr. Miller was an extremely dominate man who held a vice-like control on his family. The Millers were buttoned up tightly, but why?

Inside the home's office, Dade tweaked John Miller's computer settings, opening up sights to porn he was certain 'ole Johnny-boy had never heard of, and from what Dade could tell, 'ole Johnny-boy had missed very few. Opening his tool bag, Dade pulled out several erotic magazines and tucked them into Mr. Miller's bottom desk drawer, and he fit a few matchbooks from local strip joint, snugly behind Mr. Miller's stack of business cards in the top-drawer pencil tray. Whistling, he stood up, brushed off the dust bunnies that now tumbled atop his work area, hid wires back into their positions, returned the pen and tape holders to where they belonged on Miller's desk and walked briskly toward the office door. Keeping his cap low over his eyes, Dade stepped out into the Miller's foyer, hollered to Mr. Miller, or whoever was in earshot, "Got you all taken care of." *Boy, do I.* "We'll send you a bill," Dade continued as he walked out the front door of the Miller family home. Wearing a smirk, he thought to himself, *this is just too easy* and laughed like a hyena. *I need more challenge, more excitement. Something to get my heart rate up.*

Chapter Forty-Eight

HONOR YOUR PASTOR

And we beseech you, brethren, to know them which labour among you, and are over you in the Lord, and admonish you; and to esteem them very highly in love for their work's sake. And be at peace among yourselves.

1 Thessalonians 5:12-13

Sunday morning had arrived faster than the new father had imagined possible. He simply wasn't ready. His sermon prep had come between midnight rockings, diaper changes, laundry, cooking and cleaning. His efforts to help his wife in her new role of mother had left him with little time to spare for crafting a message for his congregation. How did women do all this? This Sunday morning he'd be shooting from the hip, so to speak, as he delivered his sermon. *Father help me!* He rushed around, picked up the diaper bag, tucked in a bottle of Heather's breast milk and a couple of extra diapers, and hollered at Heather again about the time and how close they were cutting it.

He could barely hear Heather's soft voice. "You go head Scott; we'll be there shortly."

We. He liked the sound of that. Nevertheless, he was exasperated and whipped over to the open nursery door, ready to deliver a brief sermonette about the importance of punctuality, solely for the benefit of his wife and child, just to get things moving along. However, once he'd arrived at the nursery's door, his eyes fell upon the loveliest sight he'd ever seen in his life. It was the picture that makes the knees of many a new father buckle and brings tears to the eyes of the most hardened criminal. There she was, his sweet Heather completely at peace, humming as she rocked and nursed their little one, precious Channah, a sacred trust. Did it get any better than this? Surely God would understand his wife's tardiness to church this morning of all mornings, but would his congregation? He quickly decided they'd just have to and said, "All right, girls, I'll see you when I see you. Darling, would you like me to go ahead and take Channah's bag to Mrs. Sweeney in the nursery?"

"That'd be great, shug," Heather said tenderly with such serenity that Scott, spellbound, had to fight the urge to pull up a stool and stay with his new little family for a while longer. He suddenly longed to rest, to take it all in, to soak up the aura and marinate in the vibes that seemed to have settled in on Channah's nursery.

Instead, he bounded out the door of their home, two steps at a time off the front porch, racing in the direction of his church, baby bag in tow. Halfway there he realized he'd left his Bible with the few notes he'd managed to jot down for today's sermon tucked inside the cover, on index cards, so he turned around, dashed back into his house, grabbed his Bible, and started again the jog to church. Hopefully, he and his little family would fall into a more efficient routine soon.

Sitting plumply in her pew waiting, Sister Joslyn looked at her watch impatiently, tapping her foot. Late, late, late. *We have schedules for a reason, Pastor*, she scolded him inside her head.

Shooting like a rocket into his church, Scott was surprised to find it already full. In fact, it was packed. Flying down the aisle toward the front, he welcomed his congregation, shaking hands as he hurried toward the pulpit. Finally, standing before his people, he wiped the sweat from his brow, "Er, uh, good morning, Church. I'm so glad you are here," he stated as he looked out across the crowd and was instantly choked up. His eyes got misty until he could hardly see. Through the blur of tears, he saw Ronny, the Sherriff's nephew, sitting next to Sally. He didn't know what he would've done if Ronny hadn't shown up when he did to deliver Channah, and the meal he and Sally brought by the house later was incredible. Good people.

There was Ruth, God love her. She and Henry were the salt of the earth. They'd been so helpful, Henry running up just after the wreck, ready to help in whatever way he could and Ruth at the house, greeting people, washing dishes, cleaning, and pitching in. They'd been a literal godsend. And of course, there was Sister Jewell. His heart swelled as he wondered what he, Heather and, in fact, this church, would have done without Sister Jewell. *Father, I'm so thankful for the many ways you have blest my family*, he prayed silently.

Just then, Matthew rose. Dear Matthew. He'd had his hands full with Willie's overdose, and yet he was here this morning in church. Matthew together with Alice. Oh, and there was Willie, smiling shyly up at him; he'd come this morning. A beginning. Together, they all three stood and worked to carefully push, balanced by way of a dolly, a beautiful walnut baby wardrobe toward the pulpit. He'd never seen anything quite like it. Was that a swath of vivid purple wood inlaid across the front doors of the cabinet? Brilliant. He'd known Matthew was a carpenter, but when had he had time to build this heirloom?

They were followed by Margaret, Brother Fredrick, and little Ben, hauling a car seat to the front of the church. Next, Sally and Ronny wrestled a highchair toward the front. Henry and Ruth carried up a baby swing. Dr. Mulligan pushed up a stroller. Everyone laughed when Sheriff McGowan and his wife brought up a stuffed elephant and laid it in Pastor Scott's arms as it sang and mechanically flopped its ears up and down. The sheriff was such a cut up that the elephant, coming from him, seemed appropriate. Jessie and Janie brought a baby bath with a big pink bow tied all the way around it, and Stephen, a microwaveable weighted teddy bear. Crib sheets, diapers and a baby crib mobile were next. On and on, gift after gift was laid on the altar as Pastor Scott's church, behaved like THE church, and showered their beloved pastor and his new little family with love.

Pastor Scott didn't know if it was due to sleep deprivation, being so touched by the people of his fellowship, or both, but tears streamed uncontrollably down his cheeks as he looked up to see Heather holding his precious little girl, standing at the back of the sanctuary, beaming warmly in his direction. Their eyes met across the room, and he knew. She'd known about this morning's showering, and his heart was suddenly about to burst with gratitude as she carried Channah toward him and stood beside him at the front of the sanctuary.

Once the altar was covered with baby gifts for Channah, Brother Fredrick said, "Pastor, we'd like to pray for you and your family," and the entire assembly, except Sister Joselyn, Richard and his wife, gathered round their pastor, his wife and child, laid hands on them and prayed.

The *Amen* was followed by Sister Jewell's announcement. "Well, now, I'd say we've had ourselves some gen-u-ine church." Smiling broadly, she continued, "Cake and ice cream await us in the fellowship hall. Is there anything more decadent than having cake for lunch?" she laughed. "What a great way to celebrate little Channah!"

Annoyed, Richard began sliding out of his pew so he could beat the crowd to Fellowship Hall and commandeer himself to the front of the line. Who did that old woman think she was, calling off church? We pay this guy to preach!

The room began to clear as congregants filtered out of the sanctuary. Before walking out himself, Henry walked up to and patted Amil on the shoulder, startling him. "Sorry, didn't mean to take you off guard, Brother. Just thought I'd see if you are gonna be able to join us for some cake and ice cream down in the fellowship hall."

Uncomfortable, Amil stammered, "No, I've, uh, got to get going," and rushed out of the sanctuary and onto the street.

As Henry watched after Amil, Sister Jewell stepped up beside him, saying sadly, "A tormented soul, that one."

Henry quietly nodded his agreement.

In the fellowship hall, Sally cut and served cake while Ronny scooped ice cream into each bowl. Silently he wondered if it was possible to dip ice cream and not end up sticky all the way up to your elbows. That question aside, he'd decided some time ago that he and Sally made a good team. In fact, he'd thought so since they were kindergarteners. When you grow up with someone and are with them all the time, you get to where that's the way it should be. You fit together. It wasn't like he wanted or needed to get to know her better. How much better could you know someone you'd always known? As far as Ronny was concerned, the two of them just belonged together; that was the simple fact of the matter.

It'd been a wonderful weekend. They'd talked deep into the night, and Ronny had enjoyed helping Sally in the café yesterday. As much as they'd laughed and jawed into the twilight, he'd not had time to talk with her about his feelings or his uncle's job offer, but working for his uncle at the Danport Sheriff's Department was in the forefront of his thoughts this afternoon as he scooped out the last of the cream and dropped it into little Ben Becker's bowl.

Before church, Ronny had packed up his gear in preparation for his drive back home later that afternoon. He knew that as he drove home, his thoughts would be consumed with the pros and cons of turning in his resignation and making a permanent move to Danport so he could be closer to Sally and how to make all of that happen.

Brother Fredrick guided little Ben to the table where Margaret waited, and Ben sat down next to his mother. Margaret wiped the dribble of ice cream from Ben's chin and looked up at Fred, who was wearing the most serene countenance as he gazed at Pastor Scott, Heather, and Channah. Sighing, he sat down, and Margaret knew without Fred saying so that he himself longed for such a life. Fred was a family man at heart, and he'd been cheated of that opportunity when his wife left him.

Across the room the Miller family sat in a tense little knot, Mr. Miller closely guarding what was his. Lauren, hair stringy and hanging in her eyes, looked down at her bowl of cake and ice cream as it liquified into soup and pushed it aside. Lola, her little sister, grabbed the bowl and asked, "If you don't want it, can I have it?"

"Sure."

Hearing her voice, John Miller's eyes darted toward Lauren in warning. Lauren immediately looked down and began to fold and roll her napkin.

Watching from across the room, Jeannie subtly elbowed her mother, and her mother joined her in watching the Miller family.

Ruth and Jeannie were both in deep thought, and their focus was obviously across the room on the Miller family. Dr. Mulligan was no fool. She watched the Pierce women as they watched the Millers. So, mystery solved. Ruth is concerned about Lauren Miller, and judging by Lauren's appearance and countenance, with good reason.

Jessie set drinks down on the table for Janie and himself.

"Thanks," said Janie. "You don't have to wait on me hand and foot."

"How about just hand then?"

"Do what?"

Laughing, he said, "Oh, nothing. I like to wait on you, Janie. Want more cake? More ice cream?"

Patting his forearm to assure him, "I'm good, I'm good. You're such a gentleman, Jessie."

"Tell my mom that when you come over for dinner Tuesday evening, okay?"

"I'm coming over for dinner Tuesday?"

"Oh, yeah, would you like to come over to the house for dinner Tuesday evening? Say, about 5:30? Mom wanted me to ask you."

Janie said, "I don't know, Jessie. Meet the family? Sounds pretty serious."

"Believe me, there's nothing serious about my family."

Giggling, "Well, alright then. I'll be there."

Stephen sat down next to Jessie. "Hey, you two. Good cake, huh?"

"It's pretty good all right," said Jessie. "What have you been up to, Stephen?"

"Oh, just taking care of Dad and Linda, or trying to anyway; you know how it is."

"Yeah. Well, actually, no, I don't," said Jessie.

"Well, I do," said Janie, "and it's a lot. I get it."

"Yeah," responded Stephen as he crammed the last bite of cake and ice cream into his mouth, "Oh, wow, there's Blake, gotta go," Stephen looked over toward the fellowship hall door to see Blake with pouty sable lips, eyes lined thickly, hair ink black and chaps. Rising from their table, Stephen said, "See ya Wednesday for Youth," and sauntered over to Blake. The welcoming committee, his hand extended, Stephen readied himself to shake the hand of the effeminately dressed young man.

Janie shook her head in amazement and wonder. How did Stephen do it? How could a guy like him with so much bad stuff going on in his personal life seem to legitimately care about someone else like that new kid, especially since Stephen, a big football jock, and that guy were as different as night and day? You'd think Stephen would be put off by Blake's makeup and all, but he didn't seem to be. It blew her away.

As if reading her thoughts, Jessie looked at her and said, "Stephen's the real deal."

"What?"

"He's not a fake or a flake; he sincerely tries to follow the teachings of Yeshua."

"Oh, where does Yeshua teach?"

"Uh, well, I guess right here," Jessie said holding up his Bible.

Janie said, "The Holy Bible?"

"Yeshua is Hebrew for Jesus, the Son of God."

Janie nodded, embarrassed.

"Hey, no need to feel funny about not knowing stuff; we're all learning."

"Okay. Seems like I've got a lot of catching up to do. I've got an awful lot to learn. That's a pretty thick book. It's daunting."

"Don't let it be. I grew up with this stuff, so I've got a little bit of a head start, that's true. Mostly, I'm just up to speed on all the *church-y* lingo, which isn't the goal. The goal is knowing Him. Janie, we're not in any hurry. If you want to learn, we will, together, and we'll take it slow."

"I'd like that. I'll try, Jessie, if you'll help me."

"We'll help each other."

Pastor Scott intentionally stood next to Willie. "It's really good to see you here. So, how've you been, young man?"

"Well, I guess all right. My throat's still a little sore from when they pumped my stomach, but I'm still breathing, ya know? Oh, well, a holy guy like you? You probably don't know." He looked down at his bowl of ice cream, embarrassed.

"Holy? Far from it. Actually, Willie, I might understand better than you ever imagined," Pastor Scott responded kindly. "Do you think you might have time to stop by my office tomorrow after school? Maybe we could go over to the drug store, get a Coke, and talk some."

"Sure, if you want."

"I want," Pastor Scott smiled.

Chapter Forty-Nine
BEFORE IT IS EASY

"Everything is hard, before it is easy."
-Johann Wolfgang von Goethe

Just out of church and back at Sally's, Ronny threw his bag in the back of his truck and turned to say goodbye to her. It'd been a good weekend, and he hated to leave. He hoped she felt the same.

"Thanks for coming, Ronny; you're a good friend. I've been pretty blue, so it was great to have you around. You really helped to lift my spirits."

"Good to hear," he said smiling, "so I was wondering how you'd feel about having me around all the time, Sally."

Sally looked up at him, surprised. "What about your job in Riverside, your home, your church, your life?"

"You picked up and left all that."

"Yeah, but I was highly motivated. When your dad is arrested for murdering your mom, you feel an unusual urgency to get out of Dodge. Flight mode is real."

Ronny smiled sympathetically. "I know it hasn't been easy for you."

"Everybody's got stuff. I'm okay."

"Oh, I have no doubt about that. You, my dear, are a survivor."

Sally laughed.

"So, you wouldn't feel like I was intruding in on your world, if I moved to Danport?"

"Seriously? What would you do here?"

"Serve and protect. I've been offered a job at the Sheriff's Department," Ronny said grinning sheepishly. That was actually my excuse for coming to Danport Friday afternoon, a job interview."

"Oh, I see," Sally looked up at Ronny slyly. "So, you didn't just come to see me?"

"Believe me, this job decision, this whole discussion *is* about you. So, what do you think?"

"I can't even find the words, Ronny. It would be wonderful to have a friend here, who really knows me. Having you here would be a dream come true."

"Great! I'll stop by and tell Uncle Jack, er, uh, Sheriff McGowan on my way out of town that I'm turning in my notice at Riverside." He leaned down and kissed Sally on the cheek.

Suddenly, with unexpected herculean strength, Sally wrapped her arms around him and gave him a bear hug that took his breath away. *Okay, I'm for sure doin' this; I'm movin' to Danport,* Ronny thought as he smiled to himself, pleased. Before he left Riverside for good, however, he planned to investigate a few more things about the murder of Sally's mother. That just hadn't sat well with him.

Sister Jewell dried the last dessert plate and put it up in the cabinet. The church's kitchen was finally tidy, and she was ready to put her feet up. *These dogs are barking*, she thought, but it was all worth it. Thinking about today's baby shower made her smile. Ruth's cake had been beautiful, and the homemade ice cream Brother Fredrick brought had been creamy and so delicious. She'd never imagined there was such a thing as homemade grape ice cream, but Brother Fredrick had amazed her again with his latest flavor. It seemed like everyone had a great time. Yes, it had all been a grand success, filling her with satisfaction and contentment.

"You still here?" Pastor Scott asked as he walked into the kitchen. "Last man standing?"

"Well, yes, so to speak."

"I'm just checking the doors, turning off lights, picking up trash, and jiggling toilet bowl handles so they won't run all night long. Ahhh, the glamorous life I lead, Sister Jewell. Few can imagine."

Sister Jewell chuckled. "True, true. I'll see you bright and early tomorrow morning, Pastor."

"I appreciate your filling in for Heather as church secretary, Sister Jewell. What would we do without you?"

Sister Jewell smiled at him. "Have a nice rest of the day, Pastor."

"Oh, we plan to. Sister Jewell, do you have a minute?"

"For you, Pastor, always."

"Well, Heather received a terrible letter. Anonymous, of course. I've had a few others stop by my office, heartbroken, because they too have received one of these nasty correspondences. It seems someone is engaged in a poison letter writing campaign."

"Hmm, yes, so it would seem."

"Got any ideas? What should I do?"

"First, let's both pray about the matter this evening, get some rest and we can discuss a plan of action in the morning, Pastor." Walking out of the kitchen, Sister Jewell added, "Right now, I've got to get home to my Snooky. I suspect he is desperate to get outside and find his spot."

Later that day, long after Ronny had left for Riverside, Sally fixed a cup of tea and sat in her window seat, thinking it might be a good time to read. After all, what were Sundays for if not rest and the reading of a good book; but instead, she began to rehash, rethink and relive. She'd been ten when her mother had been diagnosed with M.S. It'd started nearly inconsequentially, an occasional stumble, exhaustion, sudden headaches. At the time they'd all thought that symptoms like those weren't particularly remarkable for a woman who was raising a family and holding down a full-time job. Dizziness often happened to the healthiest of persons if they stood up too quickly. How could any of them have known? In the end, they learned the hard news that it was more than just the stress of an active life. The symptoms added up and were identified as muscular sclerosis. During the decade that followed,

Sally watched her mother fight to maintain her dignity while grappling with health issues that would test the most optimistic of hearts.

When it had been time for Sally to go back to graduate school, she'd not wanted to leave, but her mother had insisted she go, claiming that it would ruin her, absolutely destroy her if she felt that she'd in anyway held Sally back. Trembling, Sally's mother insisted on doing the pinky finger oath with Sally, and made her promise to fly, to soar, to do the things she could no longer do, live large. It was hard to listen to her mother struggle to speak, slurring her words with her muscles jumping and deny her anything, and so Sally had complied. Two days later, her mother was gone. They'd found her wheelchair tipped over at the edge of the pool and her mother at the bottom. This was shocking in itself, but also, the pool was an area that her mother couldn't have gotten to on her own in her condition, or so everyone thought. Enter the homicide investigation and her father's eventual guilty verdict. It's always the spouse, right?

Sally had tried to support her dad, tried to believe him when he said he didn't do it, but then how? How had it happened? Ronny had always believed Daddy was innocent. It amazed her, the faith he had in her dad. She shook her head in bafflement. It would be nice to have Ronny in town. She couldn't believe he was really going to move here, to Danport.

She watched the street below as she drew a long drink from her hot cup of Earl Grey. Who was that on the sidewalk? It was Amil. That guy was in her café often enough that she recognized him even from this angle. Who was he listening to? Why was he so distressed? His shoulders were taught and slumped; he looked defeated. Who was there with him? Who was Amil seeing? No one. There was no one there, just air, and yet Amil was obviously hearing someone; he was clearly being hurt as if he was suffering terrible pain inflicted by someone there with him. He seemed to see his tormentor vividly.

Dade cackled at Amil. Squealing with delight, he mocked Amil's struggle as he pinched him, scraped, pressed, squeezed, pressured, weighed on, and constricted him. *Dark. No way out.* He whispered thoughts into Amil's mind without actually speaking them. *Trapped.*

Hopeless. Death. Now. Do it, Amil. Hurry. Move. Get it done. Ruin. Spoil. Demolish. Destroy. It is your only way out. End this. Amil's bottom lip curled as he felt the pain of forceful pressure points. His skin was plucked and tweaked, pricked and bruised. Scratches raked across his chest, and the smell was unbearable as if something decomposing was squeezing the wind from his lungs. His head throbbed, his ears pounded, so loud, so loud. He questioned whether his eyeballs would pop, the pressure was so intense, was he having a stroke? Nausea churned his belly. He'd reached his limit. He wanted to die, to make it stop. Just as Amil was about to scream in anguish, Dade blew him a kiss, waved his fingers at him, and was gone. Amil crumpled against the lamp post, drained, exhausted. He couldn't take it much longer. He'd reached his breaking point.

Chapter Fifty

OLD THINGS ARE PASSED AWAY

Therefore, if any man be in Christ, he is a new creature: old things are passed away; behold, all things are become new.
2 Corinthians 5:17

Time slows for no one, and by Monday, Sally was in the fast lane again and back in her routine. She closed the café's door after her last lunch customer. Finally, she had a moment to sit down, put her feet up and sort through her mail. Bills, bills, bills...what's this? Sitting up, setting her feet on the floor, she opened the letter, which had no return address. Its contents caused her eyes to sting. After reading further, she dropped the letter into her lap and buried her face into the crook of her elbow on the table. How had this happened? Her secret was no longer a secret. Someone knew. It was out.

After school, Willie slowly walked to Church. Stepping into the lobby, just outside the offices, his eyes met Sister Jewell's as she answered the phone, "Good afternoon. Community Church. How may I help you?"

Willie nervously slunk into the office's seating area and took a seat in one of the chairs. He'd barely gotten comfortable when Pastor Scott opened his office door and popped off, "Willie, there you are. Ready? Let's walk over to the drug store and get a Coke. Maybe a Snickers. I could really use a sugar rush about now. Sometimes I get so sluggish in the afternoon, don't you? Coming?"

They walked out the church's office doors and headed toward the drug store where Pastor grabbed a king-sized Snickers bar from the rack of candy and asked Willie, "Want anything?"

"Yeah, maybe some Sour Patch Kids."

"Whew. I don't know how you eat those. Makes my mouth pucker just thinking about putting my tongue on one," he laughed. "What would you like to drink?"

"How about a Root Beer?"

"Sounds great. June, make that two," Pastor Scott said to the lady behind the counter as he pulled out a couple of bills.

"I can get mine," Willie dug into his pocket for some cash.

"Absolutely not. Thank you, but no. Let's sit over there, Willie."

Willie followed Scott and together they found a booth that seemed a little more secluded than the others. "Thanks for meeting with me, Pastor."

"My pleasure, Willie. I'm so proud of you for coming to church yesterday and all. Sometimes the first step is the hardest."

"Yeah."

"Well, I promise, it'll get easier. I know that for a fact. Willie, I wanted to visit with you because I'd like to share with you, my testimony. I don't talk about it a lot, but I think in your case, it might be good for you to know. It might help you to know that your Pastor was once a homeless junkie."

"What? No way!" Willie looked aghast at the prim and proper clean-cut man, wearing a gingham shirt, sitting across from him in the drug store booth.

With that opening line, Pastor Scott went on to share with young Willie his story of deliverance, ending with, "...so you see Willie, it is possible. You can kick this, and I will be with you every step of the way, if you'll have me."

Willie stared at his pastor, stunned. Never in his wildest dreams had he visualized Pastor Scott with such a background.

At that moment, a bearded man with a ponytail and a sleeve of tattoos on both arms walked up to their booth. Trotting close to his right calf was a Belgian Malinois. Pastor Scott stood smiling broadly at the man and then they embraced warmly. "James. Thanks for coming. Here, have a seat next to me." As the man sat down, Pastor Scott said, "Willie, I'd like to introduce to you the man who literally saved my life; oh, and this is Sgt Nubs," he said addressing the dog at James' feet, "both retired military. James was Sgt Nubb's handler when they served together in the USMC K9 Unit. I took the liberty of inviting them to join us today. I hope you don't mind?"

Willie shook his head but was obviously a little uncomfortable.

"Willie, this is the street preacher I told you about, James, the man who found me in the alley sleeping under a cardboard box with greasy hair down to my shoulders, filthy rags I called clothes, and, I'm sure, body odor that must have stunk to high heaven."

James laughed, "And beyond."

"James fed me, cleaned me up and told me about Jesus. After that, every time I relapsed or had a meltdown, he was right there to help me. He mentored me in scripture, helped me get a job. I owe this man my life."

James reached across the table and shook Willie's hand. "Willie, it is an honor to meet you," he said with the kindest eyes Willie thought he'd ever seen.

"Thank you. It's, uh, it's nice to make your acquaintance."

Pastor Scott laughed. "I know this is a lot, Willie, but I just, *we* just wanted you to know that you've got a support team if you want us. James and I are going to help you through this, I mean, if that's what you want."

Just then, June brought a gigantic root beer float with piles of whipping cream and sprinkles and set it in front of James. Scott and Willie both looked at James, surprised that a slim guy like him could put away something so massive. "When you said to me over the phone that you were buying, Scott, I thought, why not?"

They all laughed.

Chapter Fifty-One

TRUTH

"Truth will ultimately prevail where there is pain to bring it to light."

-George Washington

In Riverside, Ronny circled the Morgan property again, walking slowly. He'd gone through the evidence box at the station so many times his eyeballs were numb. He'd stepped through the Morgan house and around it so often that he now knew it was 212 paces around and 18 paces across the house. Even with that, he kept coming out here, searching for something. Anything. He just couldn't shake the nagging feeling that he was overlooking something. He was missing something. He'd felt from the very beginning that Mr. Morgan simply couldn't be guilty; he just had to be innocent. Ronny had grown up around this family, he'd spent a lot of time in this home, and he knew Mr. Morgan to be a very good man, a man like that didn't murder the woman he'd loved for 24 years. Ronny thought of all the times he'd hung out with Sally here in this home. He'd been envious of what Mr. and Mrs. Morgan shared, the love and trust they had for one another. Theirs was a romance for the ages. Nope, that wasn't something a person could pretend or fake; it had been real. Mr. Morgan had been genuinely in love with his wife. He knew how hard her diagnosis had been on Mr.

Morgan, how he'd grieved. It had been tough on the whole family, the whole community. Everybody loved the Morgans. Mrs. Morgan had been so brave and determined not to be a burden, but as her conditioned worsened and she required more and more constant care, Mr. Morgan never acted as though she encumbered him in the least. He remembered Mr. Morgan telling him that it was his honor to care for his beautiful bride. No, this was not the kind of man who would murder his wife--Ronny was certain of that. He just needed proof. Surely, if he kept digging, he'd find the answer.

Just as he walked around the corner of the house, headed toward the pool in the backyard, the sun glinted off of something in the air. It was something flying. What was that buzzing about up there? Was it a drone? Hurriedly he tried to keep track of it, to follow it. Who was controlling it? Were they nearby? It lifted and swooped to the west and then took a hard turn toward the north. Running, trailing it, so far Ronny had been able to keep up with it. There it was descending into that backyard across the street from where he now stood. Wasn't that the Russell's place? He lifted himself over their fence and jumped down into their backyard, landing with a thud on all fours. He looked up eye level with the little Russell boy, Laurence, who was holding his shiny drone and the controls. Next to him were the massive hairy legs of the man Ronny assumed was little Laurence's dad. "Hey there. Laurence, isn't it?"

Laurence just gawked at him with saucer eyes, "Who are you, mister?"

In a sterner voice, *Hairy Legs* asked, "Yes, just who exactly are you and what are you doing literally dropping into our backyard?"

Ronny raised himself up, cleared his throat as he brushed off his trousers, and responded, "I'm with the Riverside Police Department, sir. My name is Ronny, Ronny McGowan." Ronny held out his credentials for the Russell men, "I'm doing some follow-up on the homicide that took place a few blocks over. The Morgan's place?"

After glancing at Ronny's identification, Hairy Legs shook Ronny's hand, pumping it up and down and said, "We heard about all that. Terrible, terrible."

"It really was. Sir, about Laurence's drone, does he fly it every afternoon?

"'Pert near. It's taken a lot of practice, but you've 'bout gotten the hang of it, haven't you, son?" he said patting young Laurence on the back. Laughing he said, "At least we haven't crashed it yet, like the others, right, son?" Then, looking with wonder into Ronny's eyes, he added, "You wouldn't believe how amazing a bird's eye view is. Of the world below, I mean."

"That's what I wanted to talk with you about, sir."

"I'm listening."

"So, you mentioned the drone and its bird's eye view, which leads me to ask, do you record any of Laurence's flights?"

"Missions, officer, we call them missions."

"Of course. Would there possibly be any recordings? Any video from Laurence's missions?"

"Maybe. Some. We're slowly getting better at that, too. Officer, follow me to the command center. We'll check it out, see what we've got."

While walking together to the back part of the Russell's house, young Lawrence asked Ronny, "You really a policeman, mister?"

"I sure am."

"Never seen a real policeman up close."

"What do you think?"

"I like your badge. Do you get to drive fast, with lights and stuff?"

"Sometimes. If it's all right with your dad, maybe I could take you on a ride sometime."

"Really? That'd be awesome. Dad?"

"First things first, son. Let's see if we can find an entry in our mission log for the day the officer is asking about," answered Lawrence's dad.

Stepping through the back door of the Russell home, the three of them entered a darkened cool room just to the right, where small round lights were blinking a rhythmic beat to a low mechanical hum and monitors that provided slight illumination. Ronny now understood why the Russell's called this the command center. Laid out before him was a pretty sophisticated set up. Two large monitors hung on the wall over a long desk on which sat two large computer screens facing two office chairs. There were two keyboards. Each one on a pull-out drawer, just in front of each chair, and two headsets with mics lay to the side. Wires were meticulously wound and tethered. A shelving unit in the corner held other drones, four to be exact. Each one had a name plate below its resting place. Dasher, Dancer, Prancer, and Vixen. Ronny assumed Laurence was holding Comet, the fifth and empty space on the shelf. Across the room on the opposite wall to the desk was what looked to Ronny to be a worktable. Two bar stools rested out of the way, tucked just under the table, which was covered with tools and had low hanging fluorescent lighting on the ready. A flip of a switch on the wall would thoroughly brighten the area. A fan turned overhead, providing needed circulation, helping to keep machinery and human alike from overheating. Mr. Russell went to a clipboard that was hanging on the wall to the side of their desk and began flipping through the pages of his records until he came to the date Ronny was interested in, the date of the death of Sally's mother. Pointing to the entry he'd been searching for; he sat down in front of a computer screen and began typing on the keyboard. Laurence carefully sat Comet in its place over its shiny gold nameplate on the shelf in the corner and joined his father at the desk.

"What exactly are we looking for, Officer McGowan?"

Chapter Fifty-Two

MONSTERS ARE REAL

"Silence encourages the tormentor, never the tormented."
-Elie Wiesel

It was late at night, or early morning, depending on how you looked at it. He'd just left her. Seething with fury and feeling horribly gross, utterly lost, her cheeks wet with tears of outrage and disgust, Lauren began to throw things into her backpack. This was the last time he would do that to her. He would never touch her again. She never wanted to even see him again. He wasn't a father, he was a monster, and she hated him with every fiber of her being. She was seething. She fumed with rage, adding to the fire in her belly. How dare he! She beat her fist into her pillow, buried her head into her clasped hands, and sobbed quietly in hopelessness.

She was leaving. No choice. She'd stayed to protect Lola, but she'd stayed as long as she could. She couldn't protect her little sister. She couldn't even protect herself. Lola would have to fend for herself. She whimpered with the sadness that overwhelmed her, thinking of what was surely in Lola's future. Raising her window, she threw out her backpack and followed it to the ground below. Strangely, she noticed the moon was full, the crickets were chirping, the world was still turning. How surreal. How could everything be ticking along so normally when her life was anything but.

She'd managed to scrounge up enough change for a bus ticket. If she hurried, she could make it to the station by five and catch the next one out of town. Climbing out her window, down the tree and on to the ground, she secured her backpack over each shoulder and began the walk through the park where she and Jeannie had sat and talked about everything but the elephant in the room, or elephant in the park, as it were. Good grief, how could she even think silly things like that at a time like this? Room? Park? Elephant? Who cares? Wasn't it strange how the mind worked? She felt this might be a good sign, or a bad one, depending on how you looked at it. She was either not taking this moment as seriously as she should, or she still had a sense of humor and might actually survive.

As she walked past the high school running track, she noticed the team training. That was dedication, to be at the track at this hour each morning. Standing at the chain link fence for a moment, she watched as the girls raced around the course. Round and round they ran to the point of nearly being hypnotic to Lauren. Unable to tear her eyes away, she stood mesmerized by the life that might have been hers had things been different, had she had a different father. She was struck by the innocence of those out on the field. They got to be just regular high school girls, learning how to put on eyeliner, whining to their mothers about having to make their beds, and giggling with their girlfriends about some nerdy boy. Unlike her, they didn't view men as suspect. They had fathers who loved and protected them. These girls did normal things like competing on the track team, things she'd never had the energy to do or been allowed to do. He'd kept her on such a short leash lest she divulge their secret. She'd stood watching too long. Jeannie had spotted her and was running over.

"Hey, friend. You're up early. You thinking about joining the team?"

"Oh, uh, no, it's probably not for me," replied Lauren.

Jeannie noticed the full backpack. Pointing to it, she asked, "Getting an early start on studying?"

"No. I gotta go. Thanks for being my friend, Jeannie."

Jeannie watched Lauren turn and walk away, curious that she wasn't walking in the direction of the school building, but towards downtown. Thanks for being my friend? That sounded pretty final, like a goodbye even. "Hey, Lauren, wait up," Jeannie called as she caught up to Lauren. "What are you packing in that heavy backpack of yours? It looks pretty full."

Suddenly, years of abuse broke through the dam Lauren had carefully constructed around her emotions in order to survive. Falling into Jeannie's arms, she wailed uncontrollably. She cried for her older sister, Trish, who'd escaped, but in the process had abandoned her. Now she understood the heartbreak of fleeing, of having absolutely no choice but to run for it, but in so doing, leaving a loved one behind, knowing. Knowing. Knowing that loved one would be his next victim. Lauren knew, just like Trish had known, the horror of what awaited her little sister. How could she abandon Lola? How could Trish have abandoned her?

Filled with compassion that wasn't her own, compassion that was beyond her capabilities, Jeannie stroked Lauren's stringy, oily hair. She was unbothered by the bad smell of Lauren, the body odor which usually kept her an arm's length away. Instead, she was overcome with sympathy. For the first time in her life, Jeannie was able to overlook uncleanness and other flaws that would normally have repulsed and turned her away. Instead, she was overcome with love. This was not a normal emotion for Jeannie. Oh, she loved all right, but it was in a surface, easy to love setting. She loved people who were clean and smelled nice. It wasn't hard to love people who didn't stink, regular people like her, who weren't odd. Jeannie was like many who'd lived a sheltered life; she was generally a little judgmental, critical. This love that washed over her now wasn't her own. It wasn't temporal. She knew in an instant this was God. Praying silently, Jeannie asked Him for wisdom.

Coach was about to holler at Jeannie to get her butt back out on the track when she noticed the exchange between her star athlete and Lauren Miller. Jeannie had long ago laid down a pattern of good behavior, training hard, being honest, an encourager, a real team player and respectful, too. That in mind, Coach decided to trust Jeannie; she'd earned it, and so she turned away and headed back toward the rest of Jeannie's teammates, banking on Jeannie to do the same and join the team as soon as she could.

Ruth pulled up to the track early, ready to pick up Jeannie from practice. She was planning on having her quiet time here in the car while she waited for Jeannie to finish up with her training this morning. She smiled to herself as she was reminded, that waiting in the car to pick up kids was sometimes the only moment, she could steal away from the chaos of her family to do such things. Sometimes it was her only opportunity to zero in on scripture. As she reached over to the passenger side of her car to get her Bible, she noticed Jeannie holding someone, a girl just outside of the fence that surrounded the high school track. They were in an embrace. The girl Jeannie was holding had on a backpack that was rocking almost comically, bumping up and down as the girl, obviously distraught and wracked with tears, wept bitterly. Just then, Jeannie looked up, noticed the family car in the distance, and said something into the girl's ear. They broke apart and started walking toward the car where Ruth sat. That's when Ruth recognized the girl with the backpack. It was Lauren, Lauren Miller and at this hour of the morning. She didn't remember her being on the track team. What was going on? Quickly, Ruth understood the significance of what she was witnessing, picked up her phone, and punched the number of one of her contacts.

"Ruth, it's early, is everything all right?"

"Helen, we need you," Ruth said into her cell phone.

"I'm on my way, I'll be at your home in fifteen minutes," replied Dr. Mulligan before hanging up her phone.

Jeannie and Lauren made it to the car. Jeannie's voice cracked as she opened the door and said, "Mom? Lauren's with me. I told her we would help her." Barely able to complete the sentence, Jeannie burst with the tears she'd been bravely holding back.

"Of course we will help. You girls get in," Ruth said. Jeannie and Lauren crawled into the car, and they turned away from the high school track and drove home.

Pulling the Pierce's family car up to their home, Ruth saw Henry waiting for them on the porch. Under the light behind him stood Helen. Seeing them on the front steps of their home, Ruth could tell how worried they were. As Ruth walked up to the porch, Henry put his arm around her and said, "Ruth, honey, what's wrong? What's going on? Helen just got here and said you'd called her."

Ruth patted his arm, assuring him by saying, "I'm fine, shug, I'm fine. Jeannie's fine. It's Lauren. She needs our help. I called Helen for Lauren."

Henry looked up just then and saw Jeannie getting out of their car with Lauren Miller. Lauren's eyes were puffy from crying; her cheeks wet from tears. Helen walked toward her as Ruth broke away from Henry. "Lauren, I'd like to introduce you to my friend, Dr. Mulligan. I believe she will know what to do to help you."

Shaking Lauren's hand, Dr. Helen Mulligan said, "It's a pleasure to meet you, Lauren. Come, let's all go inside," she concluded, placing her hand respectively on Lauren's back just between her shoulder blades, guiding her up the front porch steps.

Ruth put her arms around Jeannie's shoulders, lining up behind Helen and Lauren, and together, they all walked into the haven of the Pierce's living room. Henry followed the gaggle of females, saying, "I'll start some coffee."

In a strangely calm and almost stoic tone, one word methodically and carefully placed after another, Lauren opened up for the first time in her life, sharing her nightmare. The barrage had been breached; there was no turning back for her now. Freedom compelled her to expose to the light her incubus, if for no other reason than to hopefully spare Lola being condemned to the same bastille in which she and Trish had been prisoner.

Jeannie was in complete horror and shock. Never in her *Leave it to Beaver* life had she ever imagined that a parent, a father no less, could hurt his own child in such a way. The tender-hearted sympathy she now felt for Lauren knew no bounds, and something else. She felt pride. She was proud of Lauren. She now understood that Lauren wasn't weak. On the contrary, she was probably the strongest person Jeannie had ever known. She was a survivor, a champion, and from here on out, Jeannie was going to do everything she could to be her most loyal supporter.

Henry and Ruth sat together, holding hands, as Lauren spoke. Their hearts ached for the suffering this precious child had endured. Henry fought to tap down the outrage that threatened to bust out of him. He was so angry. Furious! Fathers were supposed to be protectors, providers, a safe place for their children. They were supposed to reflect the love of Father God to their children. The perversion he was listening to as Lauren spoke caused bitter rancor to rise in his throat. He served at church with Lauren's father. How could that man have been leading this double life, this abomination?

Dr. Helen Mulligan listened thoughtfully with her whole being, never taking her eyes off Lauren as if she were the only person in the room. Once Lauren was through telling her story, Dr. Mulligan spoke for the first time. "Lauren, you've been very brave this morning. It's taken real courage to tell us all of this. I'm very proud of you, we all are." The others in the living room nodded their agreement. "The challenge for you is going to be to stay the course, see this to the end. I'm not going to lie to you; it isn't going to be easy. If you choose to finish this, today won't be the last time you'll be required to tell this story. In fact, if you want to change things for your family, you are going to have to retell this story many times to many different people, and there will be other tough decisions you'll have to make. I think you are strong enough and can see this to the end; plus, you have a great support system." She waved her hand around the room indicating the Pierces. "Lauren, if you are in agreement, I'd like to call Sheriff McGowan and ask him to join us here this morning."

Unsure, another tear dribbling down her cheek, Lauren stalled, "I don't know."

"I understand your hesitancy. This is your dad, your family. You're worried about upsetting your mom, you are unsure about disrupting things, but to fix this, we're going to have to do surgery and sometimes operations get messy before they heal up and get better. In your heart, you know that what your father has been doing is wrong and must stop. You've done nothing wrong, Lauren; in fact, you did everything right by coming here tonight and exposing this. Talking with us is the first step, but there will be many more difficult steps. I'm not going to sugarcoat anything for you. It's going to be uncomfortable, awkward, and difficult, but we'll help you see this to the end. We're not gonna leave you. You don't have to face this by yourself. You're not going to be fighting this alone anymore."

Lauren slumped into Dr. Mulligan's arms. There were no more tears, she'd cried herself dry. There was only absolute surrender. Exhaustion. At last, she could rest, she could lean on someone else, and she willingly yielded. "Yes, call the sheriff."

There were police cars, lights flashing and officers all around. Neighbors stood out in the street gawking curiously at the Miller home, wondering what on earth was going on. Lauren stood with Ruth, Jeannie, and Dr. Mulligan as Sheriff McGowan walked her father out in handcuffs, his head hung in shame, sobbing in utter humiliation. His sin exposed to the light, and as is so often the case, the roaring threatening lion he had once seemed to Lauren, was in reality, toothless.

Lauren searched for her mother, hoping for understanding, comfort. When the police finally withdrew and she walked with Dr. Mulligan into her family's living room, she found her mother sitting, broken hearted, in their wing back chair. "How could you? How could you?" her mother screamed as she lurched across the room toward Lauren. Henry held Mrs. Miller away from Lauren, and she fell into his shoulder wailing, "How could you Lauren? You've destroyed everything! You've destroyed our family!"

Dr Mulligan held Lauren, assuring her she'd done the right thing and that none of this was her fault.

It was at that moment, Jeannie noticed little Lola, hiding behind the sofa. Going over to her, she reached out her hand and pulled the little girl into an embrace. "It's going to be all right, Lola. It's going to be all right now. Your sister has been very brave and has saved you. We're here. We're going to help you."

Chapter Fifty-Three
SILENT NIGHT

"Silent night, holy night, all is calm, all is bright..."
-Joseph Mohr

Ruth finally got Lauren and Lola settled in the attic bedroom. She and Henry had never finished it completely, but it would do nicely until they could figure something out. She thought the girls would be very comfortable on the blowup mattresses Helen had brought over. "Why on earth did you just happen to have two twin blow up mattresses, Helen? And Serta blow up mattresses, no less," she laughed as she handed her friend a cup of fresh coffee.

"I've got a few secrets even you don't know about, Ruth."

"Oh, do tell, please do tell."

"Well, I've taken up camping."

"What? No way. You? That seems impossible!" Ruth snorted she laughed so hard.

"Please," Helen feigned offense, "I'll have you know, I'm quite capable and besides, it's such a contrast from my day-to-day life that it has become a sabbatical for me of sorts. It's a time for me to recharge."

"So do you actually have a tent, a camping stove and all the camping gear?"

"I certainly do. You'll have to go with me sometime. You can't imagine how invigorating it is."

"I stay pretty invigorated just trying to get my crew off to school on time each morning, but thanks," Ruth chuckled and then took a sip of coffee. "Helen, what are we going to do about Lauren and Lola? What's next?"

"Well, while you were getting the girls settled upstairs, I visited with Sheriff McGowan. Mr. Miller has been booked into County and will go before Judge Weary, Tuesday. The Sheriff and I agreed that it would be best for the girls to stay here with you and Henry for the time being, where they feel most safe and comfortable. They've both been through so much."

"Breaks my heart, Helen."

"Ruth, are you sure about letting the girls stay here? You and Henry already have so much."

"Henry and I discussed it, and we insist. We'll make it work."

"You haven't changed a smidgeon, Ruth. You've always taken the weak and wounded in under your wing, even when we were kids. I remember watching you feed that baby rabbit with an eye dropper. Whatever became of Thumper?"

"He lived a long full life, Helen. His grandchildren now nibble on my garden's lettuce and carrots. You'd think Thumper would've taught them to show a little more gratitude and respect."

Helen grinned and put her empty coffee cup down on the coaster. "I'd better go. Don't cook breakfast in the morning. I'll bring it by bright and early, say about 6:30?"

"Perfect."

Ruth walked her friend to the door and thanked her again. Helen responded, "It's what I do, Ruth, but it is also my heart. Balm to me. It is good, edifying for me to mend the broken hearted, if I can. Sometimes it doesn't work out like I hope it will. Too much damage. Most of the time it's a very slow process, but I'm going to try my best."

"You know I'll be praying."

"Of that I'm certain. See you in the morning."

Chapter Fifty-Four

CAMPING

"I go to nature to be soothed and healed, and to have my senses put in order."

-John Burroughs

They'd finally gotten the tent pitched, and Jeannie and Lauren sat across the campfire from Helen. She'd thought it might do Lauren some good to get outside and had picked her favorite campsite for the occasion. They weren't too far from town in case Lauren became overwhelmed and needed to return, but they were far enough away that there were no highway noises or streetlamps.

Lauren wanted Jeannie to come camping with them. So yesterday after school, Dr. Mulligan and Jeannie had gone for a peach Sprite. "Jeannie, thank you for agreeing to tag along tomorrow with Lauren when we go camping. I think maybe she considers you a friend."

"Well, I gotta admit, I'm not much of a camper, but I want to help Lauren if I can."

"You understand, Jeannie, that helping Lauren may be a very long journey. More than likely, this will not be a quick fix."

"Yeah, Mom's been peppering me with all of her wisdom," Jeannie complained.

"Don't be too quick to dismiss her. Your mom's a pretty smart lady. I'm glad she's been providing you with some guidance."

"Oh, I guess," Jeannie's voice lifted at the end of the last word.

"Jeannie, I also want to make sure you understand that you may hear some very ugly details. Should Lauren decide to open up, it could get messy really fast."

Jeannie looked at Helen nervously.

"Do you think you can handle all that?"

"Gee, Helen, I don't know. I've just never thought about a guy, much less a dad, her dad, behaving that way. Hurting her like that. Guess I've been pretty sheltered," Jeanie mused, looking down and feeling naïve.

"Nothing wrong with that, Jeannie. Your life is the way it should be. You've got great parents, a wonderful family. It's just that for some people; life's not like that. Things can get very complicated."

"Why does it have to be that way? Why can't everyone have what I have?"

"You are asking a question I can't answer, except to say that we live in a fallen world. I've talked with your mom to make sure your continued involvement with Lauren, and all of this, is all right with her."

"What'd she say?"

"She said she thought that since you'd come this far, she figured you'd want to see it to the end, that you were loyal like that. She thinks you are mature enough, Jeannie, but also recognizes, like you said earlier, you've had a very protected life, so she said that it was really up to you, shug. It may be the hardest thing you've ever done, and it'll have to remain confidential. I mean you can talk with your mom, of course, but we will want to shield Lauren from public scrutiny as much as possible. It's going to be really tough. You'll need to stay prayed up. Are you in?"

"I guess," Jeannie said looking uncertain.

"Should you decide at some point that you can't take it anymore, talk to me, Jeannie, all right?"

"All right."

Now, here they were camping, listening to crickets chirping, gazing at the stars, and spearing weenies to roast over the campfire. Their discussion veered to tomorrow's hike. They decided they'd leave after breakfast in the morning.

Jeannie asked, "Is it a difficult trail, Dr. Mulligan?" Even though she'd known Helen her entire life and had always called her Hellen, she'd agreed to call her Dr. Mulligan when around Lauren since this was a session although it sure didn't feel like one, she thought, as she slapped the mosquito that had just landed on her neck. Before Helen could answer Jeannie's question, Jeannie asked, "Where's the bathroom out here?"

Helen pointed to the trees.

Jeannie looked at her in shock. "You're kidding, right?"

Helen handed her a roll of toilet paper. "Nope."

Jeannie groaned, rolled her eyes, and snatched the toilet paper from Helen's hand, trudging off to find a tree she could hide behind. Lauren and Helen burst with laughter.

Chapter Fifty-Five

ILLUMINATION

But everything exposed by the light becomes visible—and everything that is illuminated becomes a light.

Ephesians 5:13

Sunday morning, Pastor Scott walked to the pulpit where he stood with a file in his grip. He opened the file and began thumbing through the vile letters tucked inside, one after another. He'd never read such bitterness, such trash. Who could've written these?

As his congregation waited for him to begin speaking, he silently prayed for wisdom. He and Sister Jewell had devised a plan of action, trusting that God would bring conviction and hopefully nip this poison letter campaign in the bud. However, it was a hard thing to address, to be so public about all of it. It was shameful. Such terrible words, and he didn't actually know who was responsible for this filth, but it had to stop. Now.

Opening his mouth, he began, "A number of us have received anonymous letters with the most venomous messages I've ever read in my life." He held up the file folder of letters. "Sickening stuff. It takes absolutely no courage at all to write and mail an anonymous letter; in fact, it is the act of a coward."

Was he looking directly at her? Did he know? Sister Joselyn squirmed in her seat, feeling extremely uncomfortable. Heated, she was sure her face was flushed. She had never been more furious. How dare he? Who did he think he was?

As if hearing Sister Joselyn's thoughts, Pastor Scott answered, "I am your pastor and want to be absolutely clear. Whoever is responsible for mailing these terrible letters," he pointed at the file, "will stop immediately. It ends today," he concluded with authority.

"Amen," Sister Jewell agreed loudly.

"Amen," joined Brother Fredrick, Stephen, Henry, and Ruth.

Coming around from the pulpit and kneeling at the altar, Pastor Scott said, "Please join me in prayer." Soon most of the church was kneeling at the front of the church. After forty-five minutes of intercession, the service ended, and the congregants began to leave the sanctuary.

Richard was aghast. He and his perfect little bride had, of course, remained properly in their pew during the prayer time. He'd not wanted to wrinkle his trousers by kneeling. Besides, he could pray seated in his pew and kneeling was so undignified, but now he found himself shocked. What? No sermon? What are we paying this guy for? No offering? Richard was all for being holy, spiritual, and all that, but one also needed to be practical as well. There were bills to pay after all. Even a church had to think about the lighting, air conditioning, and water expenses.

Chapter Fifty-Six
THE WOOD FAIRY

"Dance like nobody is watching, love like you've never been hurt."

-William Watson Purkey

Homecoming was here. After the football game, the dates waited in line to turn in their tickets and enter the gymnasium, which had been decorated to look like an enchanted forest. The sophomores were the servers and had been instructed to dress up as wood fairies, which made Jessie laugh. Never in his life had he imagined big 'ole Willie wearing green tights and a sequined suit that looked like it had last been worn by Peter Pan. This was great! He'd have to take lots of pictures. He gave Mrs. Holden, the teacher sitting behind the registration desk, the two tickets he'd purchased for Janie and himself, and together they walked through the streamers into the enchanted forest, pausing only briefly for their photograph in front of the trickling fountain. When they'd pulled up to the gym outside earlier, Jessie had heard the music thumping, so once actually inside, when he turned to Janie to speak, he found himself screaming, "Would you like something to drink?"

"Thank you. Yes," she shouted back with a twinkle in her eyes. She looked beautiful tonight, and Jessie felt proud to have her as his date.

At just that moment, Stephen walked up with Jeannie on his arm and Lauren on his other arm, raising his voice, "Hi, guys."

Jessie bellowed, "I was just going over to get us something to drink. Want to join me?"

"Sure," Stephen responded loudly, attempting to be heard over the music, and off they went to the refreshment table.

Jeannie shouted at Janie and Lauren, "Hey, guys, want to go sit over there?"

"Sure," they screamed together.

As the three girls took their seats at one of the round tables, they watched the dance floor, which at the moment was pretty empty. The disco ball hanging over the floor caused glimmering lights to shimmer and reflect on the vacant space. It would probably take a while before anyone would get the courage to actually dance. The dance floor remained barren.

Suddenly, the Temptations' *Ain't Too Proud to Beg* began, and the head wood-fairy glided out onto the dance floor sliding in the stocking feet of his green leotards. It was Willie, and no one had ever seen anything like it. The boy could dance and did. The party was on. Dragging Susie out onto the floor with him, Willie cocked his little green hat and began to pantomime the lyrics to her: *love so deep in the pit of my heart*. Uninhibited, Willie was completely out of his skin, dancing like nobody was watching, but of course everyone was watching. No one could take their eyes off him. That kind of bold silliness is contagious and tends to break the ice. Before the Temptations ended with *Baby, baby, baby, baby, sweet darling*, Jessie was swaying to the music with Janie, and Stephen was doing some pretty smooth moves with both Jeannie and Lauren out on the floor. Thanks to Willie, the night was not lost. The dance floor was packed and hopping.

Chapter Fifty-Seven

ALL FALL SHORT

For all have sinned and come short of the glory of God.
Romans 3:23

It was Sunday after the dance and Pastor Scott commented on how amazing he thought it was to see so many of the Homecoming attendees present in his morning service. He knew they'd all had a late night. Of course, Stephen and Jeannie were there; they didn't miss. Stephen had made a point to include Lauren when picking up Jeannie, Pastor Scott noticed. Stephen probably didn't know Lauren's story but was sensitive enough to notice she'd moved in with the Pierce family. Sitting together on the next row was Jessie with Janie. Willie and Susie were behind them and, oh, my goodness, was that Blake?

In his gut, he felt a stirring. Was this the beginning of an awakening? For a moment he was tempted to forgo the sermon he'd prepared and take the easy route, pacify Richard and maybe not ruffle any feathers. He didn't want to rock the boat. He liked living in Danport, had a new baby he'd hoped to raise here. Besides, he didn't want to miss out on a genuine movement of God, but would it really be a genuine movement of God if he didn't follow Holy Spirit's leading this morning? No. Obedience wasn't always easy, but he'd learned a long time ago, it was symptomatic of loving Jesus. He came around and stood in front of the pulpit, opened his Bible and said, "Please turn in your Bibles to 1 Corinthians 6:10-11. Let's stand together for the reading of God's word."

As the rustling of pages flipping was heard all through the small sanctuary, Richard thought again about his recent conversation with Pastor Scott, urging him to address the new kid who'd started coming to church. Blake, they called him. He smugly glanced over at the young Williams' boy. Oh, that kid was in rare form this morning with his painted nails and black lipstick. *Wait until you hear this morning what my church thinks about you, young man, or girl, or whatever you are.*

Once silence settled over the room and everyone was on their feet, Pastor Scott began, "Or do you not know that wrongdoers will not inherit the kingdom of God? Do not be deceived: Neither the sexually immoral, nor idolaters, nor adulterers, nor men who have sex with men, nor thieves, nor the greedy, nor drunkards, nor slanderers, nor swindlers, will inherit the kingdom of God. And that is what some of you were. But you were washed, you were sanctified, you were justified in the name of the Lord Jesus Christ and by the Spirit of our God, 1 Corinthians 6:10-11." With that Pastor Scott closed his book and sat down on the step. "Take your seat, guys, and close your eyes. I want you to think for just a moment. Which lifestyle behaviors listed in that passage stood out to you? Which one screamed at you? Which one has a spotlight shining on it? I suspect there's one, there's only one that you really heard when I read it out loud, but guess what? There are nine. You, if you're like many of us, you mentally grade or put a degree on sin. This sin is worse than that one. Or you think to yourself, at least I'm not guilty of such and such, that sort of thing. In the list I just read to you, there is probably one particular sin you are expecting my sermon to address this morning. As discussed, we pick and choose. Well, I hate to disappoint you if that's the case, but today I'm going to address the heart, your heart, and mine." The pastor quickly flipped the pages of his Bible to Jeremiah: "The heart is deceitful above all things, and it is extremely sick; Who can understand it fully and know its secret motives? That's chapter 17, verse 9 of Jeremiah, if you're taking notes."

Richard squirmed in his pew, cleared his throat, and looked pointedly at the pastor.

Pastor Scott didn't miss Richard's message, but pressed on anyway, basically signing his own death sentence. "The last line in the passage we read earlier from 1 Corinthians says that you were justified in the name of the Lord Jesus Christ. Why would the Apostle Paul add that to that list of sins? Because we need justification. We *all* need justification. We are reminded in Romans that we all have sinned and fallen short of the glory of God. There is none righteous, no not one. So, here's this morning's message. One sin is enough. It only takes one, just one sin to keep you out of heaven. Anyone of those listed in 1 Corinthians or a countless list of other sins will do. Sin is sin in God's eyes, and none of us are good enough on our own. But God. Except for God, we are all doomed. You see, because none of us can hit God's mark of perfection, God sent His Son, our justification. God loved this world, as rotten and filthy as it is, and provided a way for us through His Son because He knew we couldn't make it in our own strength. We *all* need Jesus, every single one of us, no matter which sin or sins you are guilty of. We all stand before God on the same playing field at the same level as sinners, and He invites each one of us to come. Come, just as you are. Would you pray with me?" With that, Pastor Scott bowed his head and began to pray.

Richard was livid. This was the final straw. No sooner was the *amen* out of Pastor Scott's mouth, than he had crushed the bulletin in his hand, tossed it down on the pew where he'd been sitting and stormed out of the church. This would not stand.

Chapter Fifty-Eight
YOU NEVER KNOW

"So, you never know who you touch. You never know how or when you'll have an impact, or how important your example can be to someone else."

-Denzel Washington

Pastor Scott heard a knock on his door. It was late. Very late. Who could be at his door at this hour? As he opened his front door, he was surprised to see Blake Williams, dressed in all black with lined eyes and black nail polish. Scott knew that Blake and his family had only recently moved to Danport from New York City. He'd noticed Stephen visiting with Blake a few times in church, and Brother Fredrick had mentioned in passing that Blake had been showing up some for Youth. Other than that, Scott hadn't really had the opportunity to learn much about the young man. Extending his hand, Scott said, "Hello. Blake, isn't it?"

"Yeah. I just have one question." He didn't shake Scott's hand.

As Pastor Scott put on and buttoned his shirt, covering a multitude of tattoos, he said to Blake, "Would you like to come inside?"

"Nah," Blake barely responded, so distracted was he by all the pastor's tats, which were quickly being covered and buttoned up. What kind've pastor was this, anyway?

"Mind if I come out, then? We can sit here on the front porch," said Pastor Scott.

"Yeah, okay, sure." They sat together on Heather and Scott's front porch steps.

The bedroom light came on behind them. Scott could hear the baby crying and knew that Heather was going to her now to nurse.

"Hey, man, you need to go?"

Looking Blake directly in the eyes, Scott asked, "What's on your mind, Blake?"

"I just wondered if you meant what you said this morning in church."

"To what in particular are you referring?"

"Look, it's all crap to me anyway, got it? I don't really believe any of it, but if it were real, if there really was a God, could I come? Someone like me? Would He take me? Me? Just like I am? Right now?"

"He took me."

"Yeah, but look at you, man. You look like somebody in the Boy Scouts, a pretty wholesome dude." That said, Blake faltered, and then as if in an afterthought, looking confused he added, "or at least I thought you were before tonight. Bro, what's the deal with all the ink?"

Scott nodded, understanding, smiled and began to share his testimony.

Chapter Fifty-Nine

TOO MANY CHIEFS

"Everyone wants to be a leader, but very few want to lead. Being a leader requires courage."

-Jon Gordon

Before the week was out, an emergency meeting of the church elders was scheduled. Leading the charge with passion, Richard had seen to it. As the day of the meeting neared, Richard was busy documenting all of Pastor Scott's flaws. Undermining the pastor was his new obsession. Of course, he wouldn't admit, even to himself, to that being his motivation. In his mind, he was saving *his* church. It had become crystal clear to him that the pastor lacked maturity and the kind of experience that came with age. He needed seasoning. Richard put together a whole list: Scott didn't properly use the pulpit, he didn't preach correctly about sin, didn't even address the sin that was an abomination, he was too casual sitting about on the church floor, he trusted the accounting of the church's money to that hick, Henry, who'd no doubt helped himself Sunday after Sunday to the offering, and Richard was just getting started.

By the time the day of the meeting arrived, Richard had managed to stir the pot magnificently. He'd dropped little hints and innuendos to several of the others, managing to successfully get the dominoes tumbling, and now, three quarters of the elder body supported Richard and stood with him, convinced of his case against the pastor and Henry. Sister Joselyn's poison pen letters had been the icing on the cake. The whole congregation was bubbling with shock, outrage, and distrust.

Amil had done his job; he'd groomed Richard and Sister Joselyn well, but there had been so much to work with. Richard already had a huge pride issue. He was legalistic, and a critical, judgmental Pharisee, so the rest had been child's play for someone with the skill set and vast experience of Amil, who'd been tearing church fellowships apart for years. Sister Joselyn had also been no *problemo*. Drop a slight here, an accusation there, a suggestion, a hint, a possibility, or half-truth and *voila!* People were so easy, especially the Richards and the Sister Joselyns. They were always there too, there was always a Richard and a Sister Joselyn in every town, in every church.

The chairman called the gathering to order as the elders got settled in the meeting room. Henry couldn't believe this was happening. Sick at his stomach, he'd thrown up before leaving the house. He'd actually been accused of taking money from the church's offering, embezzlement. The whole thing was making him sick. It helped to know Pastor Scott had his back, believed in him and that Ruth was home praying.

"Gentlemen, we've called this emergency meeting tonight to discuss a few things that have recently become concerns for some of you. Brother Richard, you may have the floor," said the chairman.

Richard stood importantly and opened his leather-bound portfolio to the typed memo he'd prepared for tonight. "Mr. Chairman, Gentlemen," he began self-righteously before launching into his endless oration. By the time he was completing his lengthy tirade, men were beginning to shift their weight back and forth, yawning, and the chairman was glancing at his watch, "...and so my esteemed colleagues, it is with great sadness in my heart that I call for an audit of our church finances by an independent accountant and the termination of Scott Barlowe as our pastor."

The chairman asked, "Is that in the form of a motion, Brother Richard?"

"It is sir." Richard's plant, farmer Conway, dressed in overalls and strategically sitting across the room, punched awake the guy next to him, right on cue, who jumped to his feet seconding the motion, which was quickly voted on and passed.

"Very well, then. We will bring these matters to the church body for a vote at our next business meeting. Gentlemen, if there is no further business, do I hear a motion to dismiss?"

As the motion to dismiss was made, Henry hung his head in despair. How could his fellow church elders think such a thing of him? How could they be so cruel to his pastor? What was happening to his church family? What was happening to his friends in this church he'd known and loved for years?

Chapter Sixty

THE MEETING

"We must never forget that Satan is always at church before the preacher is in the pulpit or a member is in the pew. He comes to hinder the sower, to impoverish the soil, or to corrupt the seed."
      -Mark Hitchcock

The church sanctuary was humming; the place was packed. Henry was stunned. He'd never seen it so full. He'd not seen this many people in the church since Easter. There wasn't an empty seat. *I guess folks came out to see the show*, he thought sadly. Sitting next to Ruth, he wondered if he should've brought his children. Was this a night that would shame them? Before the night was over, would they be embarrassed that he was their father?

But Ruth had insisted, "We're a family, Henry. We stick together. They may be young, but don't discount your children's ability to pray for you, support you and love you unconditionally," and so they were all here, his entire tribe, all sitting in a row beside their mother, beside him.

The chairman of the elders called the meeting to order and asked Brother Richard to share his motion, which he triumphantly did, relishing his moment in the spotlight. Once he'd finished and his motion had been seconded, right on cue, the chairman asked if there was any discussion.

Brother Fredrick stood and began to defend Pastor Scott and Henry. He'd barely gotten his opening remarks out of his mouth when Sister Joselyn jumped up and screamed, "Fornicator!"

Stunned, Brother Fredrick was left speechless, wondering from where that had come. Clearing his throat, he said kindly, "Sister Joselyn, I'm not sure to whom or to what you are referring, but I'm here now to state my irrevocable belief in and support of our pastor and of Henry."

Richard pounced to his feet and shouted, "Sit-down, sit-down, you deviant!"

Confused, Brother Fredrick slowly took his seat.

At this, the dam broke, and the church erupted into total chaos, an outrageous uproar, complete with arguing and tears. It was as if they'd left their Christianity at the door. Who were these people? Pastor Scott thought as he shook his head mournfully.

Amil sat in the back pew, satisfied he'd accomplished his goal, but at the same time, very sad. Yes, mission accomplished, another church destroyed. Visible only to Amil, Dade was standing on top of the pulpit, prancing as he cackled like a hyena. That was it. Amil had all he could take. He stood to walk out when he noticed movement at the front of the church. Turning, he stopped to watch.

So far only words had flown, but they were just moments away from actual fists being thrown when Sister Jewell rose quietly and stepped up to the front of the church where she stood waiting for the church to settle down. When people finally began to take note of her standing stoically before them, they looked back and forth at one another, eventually sitting down, tucking their heads, glancing off to the side and behind them almost as if they were ashamed, embarrassed. Without raising her voice, Sister Jewell stood fearlessly and waited a good full minute, letting the silence settle.

"Be still and know that I am God," she heard His spirit whisper into her inner ear. So, she waited another minute before calmly beginning. She started with a name, then another. She named off one and then the next as if reading from a list, but she had no notes. One after the other. Just names from the church membership roster, but somehow the full pronouncement of each person's guilt weighed heavily upon those named, one at a time out of her mouth. One by one she listed off the names of the members of Community Church, and as she did, their ears heard the accusation, the sin that accompanied it. Everyone was guilty. None were righteous, no not one. Godly remorse, the kind that leads to repentance, began to fall on the entire congregation. In one fell swoop, each member of Community Church began to weep and cry out to God for mercy, so great was their conviction. Everyone in the congregation but Richard and Sister Joslyn that is.

Wait. What? No. Stop. No. No, Dade screeched in his head. At that he poked Sister Jewell hard, digging his finger in, he twisted it into her back just under her shoulder blade. He finished it all off by squeezing the chest cavity around her heart firmly, right in the middle of her recitation. Sister Jewell grabbed her chest and looked up. Heaven seemed to open up, and Sister Jewell appeared radiant, spotlighted, as if she were glowing. What, who did she see? Noticing her distress, Pastor Scott rushed to support her as he hollered for Heather, his wife, to call an ambulance.

Richard was deflated. The meeting had ended abruptly with Sister Jewell being loaded into the ambulance. That was it for now. No church-wide decision about Pastor or Henry had been made, no actual vote taken, but Richard was not deterred, he wasn't conquered. This was only a temporary setback.

Finally at home, Richard eased into his recliner, resting his head back. In the dark he stared at the ceiling. Tonight, had not gone at all as he'd anticipated. Rehashing each moment of the meeting, he was unexpectedly shaken back to the here and now by clapping. Richard looked toward the applause where he noticed, leaning against his living room wall, barely discernible, the figure of a lean silhouette who was methodically, rhythmically, giving him a standing ovation. Faster than lightening, Richard raised straight up in his recliner and screamed like a girl.

The gloomy outline of Dade only laughed at him. "Shh, shh, hush now, my pet; don't hyperventilate. I just thought I'd stop by to congratulate you, my dear," it breathed in an indistinct rasp.

"Fo, fo, for what? Who are you?" Richard stuttered, his voice getting higher with each word.

"Why, Richard, my sweet, I'm the one you serve," quipped the shadow, "and tonight was your best performance yet. Bravo!"

"SERVE! I don't serve you, whoever you are. I go to church regularly, I'm an elder; why I even go to the Prayer Room once a week."

"Yes, my beloved, you do *do* a great many things. You do a great deal," hissed the shape in agreement. "Tsk, tsk, not to feel too badly, my boy, busyness is a common snare," he added, while cleaning one of his fingernails. In an afterthought, the demon gloated, "I've snatched so many that way over the years."

"Get out of here! Get out, in Jesus' Name!"

At this, the pungent figure stepped forward, slapping his knees. It bent over in wickedly boisterous guffaws. As if it was under a beam, Richard was now able to make out its ghoulish features, contorting in unholy laughter. Catching its breath at last, Dade gasped, "And said so authoritatively, my love. I'm impressed. Not!" Dade winked. "My dear boy, Sister Jewell I know, Pastor Scott I know, why I even know that handyman, Henry, the one you've nicknamed Hick, but who are you to speak to me in the Name? Just exactly who do you think you are against me? What possible authority could you entertain over me?" Dade paused for effect. "I own you."

Richard withered, shrinking into his recliner, back pressed against the leather as Dade slithered toward him slowly, with measured steps.

Chapter Sixty-One

RELENTLESS

...take no thought beforehand what ye shall speak, neither do ye premeditate: but whatsoever shall be given you in that hour, that speak ye: for it is not ye that speak, but the Holy Ghost.
Mark 13:11

Richard was now a man possessed. Relentless, he'd been unable to let the matter die. A week later, as soon as he could orchestrate another church meeting, he was back on task and brought up his motion regarding the pastor and Henry again, "It is long overdue," Richard declared as he took the floor. "He's got to go. Obviously, we have been saddled with a man who is too young for the responsibility of a church as robust as ours. Scott Barlowe is a man too preoccupied with family matters and everything but the needs of this fellowship. He lacks the seasoning a mature and grounded congregation like ours has come to expect in a pastor. Now I will be more than happy to fill in as interim pastor while we begin another search for the appropriate man of God-dah ordained to lead and inspire us. I put that in the form of a motion."

Blustering, Sister Joselyn quickly seconded Richard's motion.

The chair asked for a show of hands. Henry leapt to his feet, "No. Wait!" All eyes turned toward the town's handyman, now standing, still in his work coveralls. "This is all moving pretty fast. It's been a while since I studied Robert's Rules, but isn't this when we should have some discussion?"

The chairman asked, "What would you like to say, young man?"

Richard snarled, "What is there to discuss? And are we really interested in the thoughts of a common thief?" With that the congregation erupted in agreement and disagreement. Everyone had something to say.

The chairman banged his gavel, "Order, order. Everyone sit down and seal your lips. Henry, you have the floor. What would you like to say, son?"

Henry hadn't actually planned on saying anything. He'd worked all day and was exhausted, but when he heard that Richard had called for another meeting, he'd rushed to the church and was on his feet objecting and asking the chairman for discussion before he knew what he was doing. As all eyes in the full sanctuary rested on him, Henry took a cleansing breath, attempting to steady his nerves. Public speaking was not his forte; nevertheless, someone had to defend Pastor Scott. Quietly, he asked Holy Spirit to give him the words to say and with that, he opened his mouth, "Our pastor may be young, but he's a good man. He's honest, loves God, studies, serves and prays. He pastors this body of believers well. Sally, when your pipes burst at the Café, who was the first person there and the last one to leave? Margaret, how many times has Pastor gone fishing with young Ben there? Willie, how many times did Pastor visit you while you were laid up in the hospital? Stephen, whose helped with your utility bills from time to time? I could go on and on. I bet each one of you has a story you could share this evening of a time when Pastor Scott or Heather reached out to you, pastored you, loved you. You could each tell your own personal story about the Barlowes and their ministry to you and this body of believers. We can't just give him the boot because we don't care for his style or..."

Sensing the tide turning in favor of Pastor Scott, Richard jumped to his feet interrupting, "I think we can all agree young Scott has made an effort. I, for one, struggle to follow his sermons, and I know I'm not the only one. I've heard others say they weren't getting anything out of his messages. He's all over the place."

High on an adrenaline rush, Henry scrunched his eyebrows together and asked, "All over the place? Are you referring to the text of his sermons?"

"No, Henry. I'm referring to the way he moves, physically moves. Literally. He's all over the place. One minute he's standing here, the next minute there," pointing from one side of the church sanctuary to the other. "We don't know where to focus. Why he's even sat right down on the steps of the platform. He exhausts me."

Shaking his head in disbelief, grieved, Henry replied, "And for that, he's got to go, Richard? Really?"

"It is an obstacle for the weaker ones amongst us. If it distracts me, a strong pillar of this fine church and community, can you even fathom what young Christians are dealing with?"

Sister Joselyn piped up, startling Henry, "Amen. Bring it." This was probably the first time he'd ever heard Sister Joselyn say an amen during a church service in his entire life.

Crouched on the church's roof top, stirring the pot with his finger in pantomime of the chaos going on below, Dade smirked, delighted with the progress of his latest recruit. Richard was turning out to be an excellent convert.

As if a puppet on Dade's string, right on cue his henchman, Richard, said, "I recently had the opportunity to visit with a new resident here in Danport, and the immaturity and lack of experience of our young pastor has taken its toll, gentlemen," clearing his throat, "and ladies, of course. Scott's methods have caused him to stumble greatly. I'm not sure he'll recover."

Amil realized Richard was speaking of him. Disgusted, he stormed out of the church. What had he done? Nothing that he hadn't done in a hundred other churches. Why did this one vex him so?

Illuminated by a full moon, Dade rolled in laughter at Richard's reference to Amil as if Amil could be screwed up any worse than he already was. Hysterical. He watched Amil charge out of the church, his face full of misery. What a hoot. Could this be any more gratifying? Tsk

tsk, poor Amil and poor, poor Pastor Scott. I'm afraid it's over 'ole boy. Another one bites the dust. This was too easy.

Beneath Dade in the sanctuary, Richard shook his fist in the air. "Scott Barlowe has got to go!"

Others stood taking up the mantra, hollering out their own grievances against Pastor Scott, imagined or real; it didn't really matter to Dade. His minions were at work, doing his bidding.

Henry watched, incredulous. Were people really this fickle? Have they lost their minds? Mayhem ensued as Henry, sick at his stomach, stared at the members of his church family. These were people he knew. People he loved. He thought they might actually come to blows at any moment. How had this happened? Did these people, his church family, leave their Christianity at the door tonight? Their crazed faces were contorted fiendishly in anger as if possessed. Something sinister was afoot. Henry knew he was out of his league. If only Sister Jewell was here tonight. He knew, even in her hospital bed, she was praying, but Henry knew if she had been here tonight, things would never have gotten this far out of control.

The chairman's gavel could be heard smacking the hard wooden surface in front of him as he bellowed, "Order, order! Please, Church, take your seats." Gradually, a false calm settled on the congregation. It was the kind of calm felt before an electrical storm whips up; you could feel the static in the air.

Continuing, the Chairman reminded, "Now we have a motion and a second to remove Scott Barlowe as the pastor of our church. Let's put it to a vote and see where we stand."

Ballots were distributed. Henry was numb. By the time the meeting ended, Henry and Ruth walked together to their home as if in a trance, neither one able to wrap their brains around what had just transpired. It was as if a tsunami had flattened their church, a church they loved. Disbelief and shock carried them to their home and up the steps of their front porch. Ruth took Henry's hand and suggested, "Henry, before we go inside to our children, let's sit out here on the swing for a spell and pray and cry," she finished as her voice cracked. "Mostly cry," and with that she began to weep.

Henry was reminded that even now in their weakness when they had no idea how to pray and could only sob in discouragement, the Spirit made intercession for them. He took Ruth in his arms and led her to the porch swing. As he held her, they began to pray in a manner that was obviously not unusual for them. They prayed on behalf of their church and on behalf of the pastor they'd grown to love, a new father and, as of tonight, a man with no way to support his young family.

Amil was curled up in a fetal position on the floor of his closet. The door was closed as if that would keep his tormentor from finding him. His mind raced. He'd been unable to slow down the storm of thoughts that created the whirlwind in his brain. He'd been raised to love God, but somewhere along the way had toyed with what he now understood to be a gateway into the occult. It hadn't seemed sinister at the time; in fact, it had almost seemed innocent like a fairy tale, children's stories, games. Books he read, the movies he saw had only fed his curiosity. And he was curious. He'd always been intrigued by such things. The dark side was his *Achilles heel*, so to speak, and Dade had recognized this weak spot and groomed him expertly.

Dade was a master at finding a person's frailties and playing on them. He'd certainly found Amil's. Amil had always been strangely drawn to dark things. Dade seemed to tune into this and invited him to what he'd labeled a party, just some friends getting together, but it'd been more than that. Way more. Hooded beings had chanted while standing around candles that lit up a pentagram drawn on the floor that night. As they droned on and on, he'd tried to figure out who was next to him but had been unable to. Diverting his attention, Dade, himself shrouded, had thrown a cloak over Amil's shoulders and immediately he'd known this wasn't the same kind of meeting his aunt attended every Sunday at Calvary Church on the corner of town. Deep inside he'd heard warning bells. He'd recognized them and known he should run, run as fast and hard as he possibly could away from this place, but the seduction had been overwhelming. He'd been hooked; like a fish, he'd been lured in. Dade described the meeting later as all fun, play acting, but Amil had known better. Even so, he'd gone to the next meeting, couldn't help himself. Time and time again he went until he was addicted.

Chapter Sixty-Two

SET FREE

...ye shall know the truth, and the truth shall make you free.
John 8:32

Sally dragged herself home from the horrible meeting at church. Climbing the stairs to her apartment over the café, she thought, *what a nightmare*! Tonight, had been just awful. She loved Pastor Scott and Heather. How could this be happening to them? Had she done all she could? She threw her keys onto the kitchen table and put water on to boil for tea. It seemed like nothing much was going right lately. She'd not heard from Ronny in quite a while. In fact, she'd begun to feel silly and a little confused about the feelings she had for him, the hopes. Had she completely misread his signals? Had there even been any signals? Perhaps she'd read too much into his visit to Danport, but she had thought he would move here and sooner than later. Instead, two weeks had come and gone; then months passed. Now it was getting close to a year. Nothing. Feeling more depressed by the minute, Sally turned off the burner under the tea kettle and decided to forget the tea and just go on to bed. Maybe, somehow, things would look better in the morning.

The sun was not yet even peeking through her bedroom curtains the next morning when Sally tumbled out of bed and began to get ready for the day. The café opened every morning at six, which meant she had to be up at five and ready to rock and roll by the time the first customer stopped in for breakfast. After putting on her makeup and tying up her hair, she pulled on her jeans and her Sally's Café polo shirt and started down the stairs from her apartment to the café. Funny, she smelled coffee and bacon. Was that really bacon? Was Cook already here?

Turning the corner of the stairs, she was about to go through the door that opened into her café when she thought she heard conversation followed by laughter. Opening the door that led into her cafe, she was blinded by the café's lights. They were already on. Wait, the lights are on in my cafe? Her eyes moved to the source of conversation, the back booth, where she saw two figures. One of them, facing her, was Ronny. He'd come. Their eyes met and immediately, every doubt she'd had fell away. She knew in an instant she'd not misread his signals. He'd come back for her, but who was he talking to? The back of the man facing Ronny looked very familiar. Just then, that man rose and turned to face her. It was her father! He was free, out of prison, but how? Behind him, Ronny had a huge grin on his face as if he'd pulled off the biggest surprise party ever. Her father's face was animated, bright with emotion, tears, and laughter all at the same time. Suddenly, it didn't matter how he was here, only that he was, and Sally flew into his arms.

After all the excitement and hugs, Sally began to ask the millions of questions bombarding her brain. Ronny systematically answered one after another. He carefully explained how the little boy's drone had filmed her mother's suicide at the pool and how he'd rushed that evidence to her dad's lawyer, who'd taken it from there. It had been a process. Taken some time. Even if you're innocent, once you're convicted and have become a prisoner, it is tough to actually get released; but finally, here he was. Her father was free; his name had been cleared. He had not murdered her mother. Sally wept with relief.

"One last question, how did you get in here?" Asked Sally.

"I picked the lock," Ronny looked down shyly, "don't tell my new employer, Sheriff McGowan."

Laughing Sally assured him, "Your secrets safe with me."

Chapter Sixty-Three

GIFT FROM GOD

Children are a gift from the Lord; they are a reward from him.

Psalms 127:3

Ruth hadn't told Henry yet. How would he take the news? Would it be too much of a burden on him? It might just be the stick that broke the camel's back. With all that was going on in their church and their personal finances ever in crisis, she couldn't imagine what he might say when she told him her news. Preparing to push the sofa out from the wall so she could vacuum behind it, all of the sudden she felt Henry behind her, gently moving her aside. "Let me move that for you, sweetheart. Sit down over there; I'll finish the vacuuming."

"Come on, Henry. Really? I can do this. Besides, you've already put in a full day's work."

"Yeah, I know. You are woman; I hear you roar," he smiled. "Ruth, what can't you do? You are a champion among women, but there's nothing wrong with propping your feet up whenever you get the chance. After all, a woman in your condition can get pretty tired. You could use a little extra rest."

"My condition? Wait, you know? How?"

Henry hugged her, laughing, "How could I not know, Ruth? After six kids, you didn't think I'd be able to read the signs? I've become an expert on expectant mothers, especially, my kids' expectant mother."

"You're not upset?"

"I'm thrilled, Ruth. Children are a gift from God."

Ruth looked at him, her face full of disbelief.

"Darling, what real man doesn't want his quiver full? My quiver is really full and seems to be getting fuller. And fuller," he joked.

"Oh, Henry, I feel like I need to apologize to you for some reason."

"You've got to be kidding. Look, I'm excited, Ruth. Besides, you didn't up and get pregnant all by yourself, madam. I mean, you had a little help." Chagrined, he raised his hand in admission. "Guilty as charged. I'm part of this equation. I am partly responsible." Henry chuckled, "We'll manage, sweetheart. Everything's going to be all right. God's been faithful so far, hasn't He? What's to think He would let us down now?"

Ruth wrapped her arms around her cowboy's waist. "I love you, Henry Pierce."

"I love you, too. Now sit over there and watch the master at work," he said, turning on the vacuum.

Chapter Sixty-Four

WEAPONS OF WARFARE

For though we walk in the flesh, we do not war after the flesh: (for the weapons of our warfare are not carnal, but mighty through God to the pulling down of strong holds;) casting down imaginations, and every high thing that exalteth itself against the knowledge of God, and bringing into captivity every thought to the obedience of Christ.

2 Corinthians 10:3-5

Grabbing his hand, Sister Jewell's eyes were tinged with desperation. "You've got to do this, Pastor. You are here in Danport for such a time as this. You can't leave. You've got to take a stand. Our weapons of warfare are mighty through God to the pulling down of strongholds and casting down of imaginations. God almighty will go before you and move on your behalf. This battle is His. I'll be holding your arms up, interceding with all my might from right here in my hospital bed. Now go, Pastor. Go."

Pastor Scott squeezed her hand, steeled himself for what was ahead of him and walked toward the door of her hospital room. Stepping outside the building, he could smell coffee brewing and bacon frying as the inhabitants of Danport began their morning, and he thought how odd it seemed. For many, it was just another day, but for him, it was the battle of a lifetime. Feeling isolated and alone, he began the short walk toward his church. As he walked, he noticed the people of Danport picking newspapers up off their lawns or peeping through the closed curtains of their windows safe inside their homes. Curious? Just plain nosy? Or perhaps anxious or even a bit wary? Maybe even a little afraid. Heck, *he* was afraid. Not every Danport citizen knew exactly what was going on down at the church, but their community was tight knit enough that they were aware that something was amiss.

There it was, just ahead of him. The church. His church. Community Church. Wait. Who was that? It was still early morning, dark and hard to see, but it looked like someone was up ahead. Someone was walking just around the corner of the church. Good grief, was that Henry? It was. Henry Pierce was walking with purpose. Concentration creased his brow, intensity measured his steps, his head was down, and his mouth was moving in prayer. Occasionally he added expressive exclamation point hand gestures and air punches. He was absorbed, lost in another zone. Stepping up beside Henry without saying a word, Pastor Scott began praying in sync with him. Henry paused only briefly, smiled, then nodded at his pastor, glad to have someone praying in agreement with him, and then they pressed on. Together they walked side by side, praying as they stepped off the length of path circling the church building.

The next morning just before sunrise as Henry arrived at the church to prayer walk, he was met by Pastor Scott and Brother Fredrick. No one said a word. They each inclined their heads in acknowledgement of one another and began their walk. The following morning Stephen joined them.

Amil awoke with a start. Bolting straight up in bed, his heart was pounding in his chest, and his body was drenched in sweat. Conviction. The dream. He'd had it again. He knew they had to be praying. Blast it! Would this never end? There was always a remnant. Rising from his soaking sheets and dragging himself to the bathroom sink, he splashed his hot face with cold water. Staring into the mirror, the feverish eyes that met his were tormented. He didn't know how long he could continue.

Behind Amil, in a dark corner, Dade eyed him from the only chair in the room. Legs crossed in an effeminate posture; he playfully swung his foot back and forth. Arching his left eyebrow, he cocked his head to the left and whispered coyly, "What's the matter, dear boy?"

Amil closed his eyes and grimaced.

"Bad dream, my sweet?"

Amil groaned but said nothing.

Blowing him a kiss, Dade murmured, "Stay strong, my pet."

Amil whipped his whole body around. Furious, he glared at Dade.

Unruffled and completely at ease, Dade playfully closed his shadowed eyes and wagged his finger at Amil, cooing through pouty lips, "Temper, temper, my darling. We're almost there."

Lunging at his tormentor, Amil screamed, "Get out, get out!"

Throwing his head back in laughter, Dade vanished.

In anguish, Amil crumbled to the cold tile of the bathroom floor, sobbing. How had this become his life?

Fresh out of the hospital, Sister Jewell rose before the sun and joined the band of prayer warriors that now, on a regular basis, walked around the church. She hobbled slowly, her cane helping to keep her steady. Each step was hard for her, but she finally made it to her church where the others were already prayer walking. Getting around wasn't easy for Sister Jewell this morning, or any morning. This was truly a sacrifice of love for her, but she knew how important it was that she be here. They were at war, this was the frontline, and she knew beyond a doubt that this was exactly where she was supposed to be. Opening her mouth, she began to pray with the others, one step at a time.

Amil thought to himself that it had never been so hard to bring down a church. The resistance had never lasted and had never been so strong. This bunch was tenacious. He'd worked in many communities, but this was the first town whose prayer warriors had stuck it out for this many months. Generally, someone would come up with the idea to pray, sure, but eventually they grew weary in well doing, their resolve would weaken, they would lose their fervor and quit. It's a fast-food world, after all. Most Christians he'd come across wanted a drive-through answer to their prayers. Place your order with God here, drive through there and pick it up. Fast, neat and efficient. Even he knew that Jehovah God wasn't some kind of genie in a bottle, waiting to have his belly rubbed so he could escape and grant a wish. If Christians knew Elohim like he knew Him, they would shudder. Generally, however, Christians were just too naïve. They didn't seem to be aware of the very real battle going on all around them. Out of sight, out of mind. Better for him he supposed. This bunch would surely give up before too much longer, like all the others before them.

Chapter Sixty-Five

STAY THE COURSE

And let us not be weary in well doing: for in due season we shall reap, if we faint not.

Galatians 6:9

Henry's alarm was blaring. Groaning, he slammed down on the snooze button, punched his pillow and rolled back over onto his side. What's the point? It's not doing any good. Nothing has changed. He drifted back to sleep and was soon snoring.

Abruptly, Henry was jarred from his slumber by pounding at his front door. Throwing his robe on he raced down the stairs. Bleary-eyed he opened the front door, "WHAT?! Oh, Sister Jewell. Sorry. I uh, well, I was sound asleep."

"I thought as much. Get your clothes on, young man. We're too close to victory now to sleep away the morning," commanded Sister Jewell.

"Close! No disrespect, Sister Jewell, but you've got to be kidding. We've been walking and praying for months now. Nothing has changed. What's the point?"

"The point? The point, Henry Pierce, is our triumph is at hand."

"How can you say that, Sister Jewell?"

"It is the way of things, Henry. Just when a person is about to give up, the breakthrough is near. This is not the time to give up. This is the time to tie another knot in that rope of faith."

Henry slumped against the doorframe, "Aren't you exhausted, Sister Jewell? I know I am," Henry's voice trailed off.

"Let us not become weary in doing good, for at the proper time we *will* reap a harvest if we do not give up. We can't give up, Henry."

"Ma'am, I've never seen faith like yours."

Chuckling, Sister Jewell patted Henry's arm and said, "Just a mustard seed, son. I've just a little seed, but it so happens, that's enough. Now go get dressed. The others have already begun."

The contingent of intercessors rounded the corner of the church just as the sun was coming up. Stopping suddenly, they came face to face with Amil. Drained, haggard, pale, with dark circles under his eyes, he looked battle worn and exhausted. Arms hanging by his side, perspiration dotting his strain-creased brow, defeated, he whispered, "Help me."

Rushing to his side, the small army supported him gently on every side. Concerned, they began to ask what they could do for him. Amil groaned, "Pray," so they did. A genuine spirit of intercession arose amongst the team. Pastor Scott laid his hand on Amil's chest. Henry laid his hands on Amil's shoulders as the others gathered round. This was not a polite little church gathering where a bulletin would establish the agenda--this was spontaneous combustion. This was outright combat.

As the warriors prayed, godly remorse washed all over Amil. Repentance followed. Sister Jewell felt it break first. The stronghold was at long last demolished. Pastor Scott grinned from ear to ear. Henry clapped his hands in delight and shouted as Brother Fredrick bobbed his head in agreement, whispering, "Amen."

Just as Sister Jewell collapsed onto the garden bench, exhausted, salty drops of tears began to tumble out of Amil's eyes. Countenance glowing, Sister Jewell lifted her gaze upward and whispered, "Thank You, Father."

The doors shut to Amil for so long, swung open wide. Amil had always deeply believed in the God of the universe and His power, but being bound, he'd forever been too ashamed to look up. Actually, raising his eyes heavenward had never seemed possible. But now, kneeling in the church's lawn with tears of joy flooding down his shining face, Amil raised his eyes toward heaven, vulnerable, exposing his face, he looked up.

It was at that moment he heard his name and thought, *this is incredible. He sees me, I know He sees me and loves me. Even after everything I've done, He loves me. Me.* Amil had been called. *Yes, Lord, I'm coming. Just as I am, I'm coming.* A warm oil-like-balm seemed to pour from the top of Amil's head to the tip of his toes. Scales that had blinded him for so long toppled away from his eyes. The clouds parted, opening to the most beautiful blue yonder Amil had ever seen. He was free. Amil laughed and cried simultaneously. Never had he thought this possible. He felt brand new. He understood that today was the first day of the rest of his life. He was a new creation. Old things had passed away. In an instant, he knew all of this and rejoiced as unseen chains plummeted away, and he raised his hands in total surrender and praise to the great I AM, the King of Kings.

Epilogue

In the same way, I tell you, there is joy in the presence of the angels of God over one sinner who repents [that is, changes his inner self—his old way of thinking, regrets past sins, lives his life in a way that proves repentance; and seeks God's purpose for his life].

Luke 15:10

Echoing from the steamy catacombs of his lair, deep down in the dark bowels of the earth, Dade could be heard snarling, his growls accompanied by the dripping and hissing of the hot springs that ran through the sauna of his headquarters. Gnashing his teeth in rage and apprehension, certain of the penalization and merciless torture awaiting him, he recoiled, brutally aware of the system and how it worked. He understood that he had failed his master, and for that he would be punished severely. Dade's jaundiced eyes squeezed closed as he collapsed in defeat. The earth trembled beneath him as he raised his serpent's face toward the dripping stalactites, opened his putrid muzzle and released a curdling howl that was heard all through the searing, dark caverns, reverberating up through chamber after chamber, rising higher and higher, until it was countered, overpowered, snuffed out, by the outrageous rejoicing and celebration underway in the presence of the God of the universe as angels raised a hallelujah because one sinner had repented. Amil, no longer bound, was free.

According to the National Sexual Violence Resource Center: 1 in 4 girls and 1 in 6 boys are sexually abused before the age of 18.

If you are victim of sexual abuse, you are not alone.
Find help by calling 1800-656-4673
(the RAINN National Sexual Assault Telephone Hotline)

Acknowledgments

Thank you to *Lil Lady Marketing and Design* for your attention to detail, the beautiful book cover, and your confidence in this project. With a B.A. in Strategic Communication and a Master of Theological Study with an Emphasis on Biblical Counseling, you're highly qualified and one sharp cookie. Your skill and professionalism in graphic design and marketing continue to impress me. You're *pretty good for a girl*.

Thank you to Editor, Shannon Cunningham. Not only a lifelong friend, but also such a kind soul that I found her gentle correction to be strangely edifying. With a B.A in English, a master's in English education, and twenty-six years of teaching experience under her belt, Shannon is highly qualified for the task of editing. She and her husband of fifty years have three children, seven grandchildren and enjoy hiking and traveling together. She is a passionate reader, dabbles at gardening and I know her to be an incredible poet.

Thank you to Quill Hawk Publishing and the Quill Hawk family for your patience, guidance, and support in transforming this manuscript into a book that is presentable and a *read* to be proud of.

Thank you to the fellow authors of Invite to Write, Southwest Indies, and OWFI where the workshops, discussions and tossing about of ideas wet creative juices, teach and provide beneficial guidance.

Last, but of course, not least, I am thankful for the encouragement and love of my husband who faithfully supports and forever inspires me to pursue writing. He believes in me, more than I believe me.

**Be looking for the next book in the Danport Series by Renée Hill.
Bound II: Soar Like Eagles**

BOUND II
Soar Like Eagles

PROLOGUE

Sitting atop the bell tower of Community Church, Dade watched the sleeping population of Danport, Vermont through jaundice eyes, as he contemplated his predicament. True, he'd bombed before, but what could he do after the deplorable bottom feeders who called Danport their home actually had the audacity to start praying in faith, and not just *mansy pansy bless me* type prayers, no indeed! They went to war. Had that not happened, the battle would've most certainly been his, he was sure of it. After all, was it really his fault? I mean, let's get real, Amil was just a weakling. Also, who would've ever dreamed Pastor Scott would still be standing. That he would stay in Danport? Much to Dade's dismay, after all he'd thrown at *Pastor Goody Two Shoes* and after all he'd put him through, that *holy roller* was still upright. Or rolling, the demon shrugged, or whatever. Never saw anything like it.

Puffing up his chest, Dade reminded himself of his own awesomeness, "You Dade are tenacious. You are still fighting the fight. You refuse to give up. You aren't a quitter. That has to stand for something." He liked the sound of his own voice

Last Fall, after his master nearly beat him half to death, because of his failure to bring down Danport, Dade suddenly felt highly motivated. A good beatin' will do that for a demon. Never failed to rev up the 'ole motor. Yep, he would succeed this time. He had to.

While the characters may have shifted and changed slightly in his story line, the battle plan remained the same; to kill, steal and destroy. Bring deception and confusion to Danport. But this time wouldn't be like before. This time would be different. This time he would be the champion. This was his time. His victory was just over the horizon; he was certain of it.

You know the old saying, *when a door closes, a window opens.* Dade pouted, Amil had been one of his best recruits, losing him broke his demon heart. It was tough and he hated to see that door close. It had been a hard squeeze, hoisting himself through the next window that opened, I mean, Richard Langley, really? But being skilled at recognizing talent, he saw potential in Richard, the little dweeb. Dade considered himself an entrepreneur, so when he saw opportunity in the person of little Richard, he seized it.

Chapter One

REMEMBER TO BREATHE

There is a time for everything, and a season for every activity under the heavens: a time to be born and a time to die, a time to plant and a time to uproot, a time to kill and a time to heal, a time to tear down and a time to build.

Ecclesiastes 3:1-3

The alarm jarred her awake. Throwing both bare feet unto the cold floor of her attic bedroom, Lauren hustled to pull on her house slippers. She'd endured years of abuse by her father, before escaping, with her little sister, to live with the Pierce's. This morning was the beginning of her father's trial. Tightening her robe, she headed for the bathroom where she splashed her face with ice cold water then turned toward the stairs that led to the kitchen. Today was the day. Before even entering the kitchen, she could smell the glorious aroma of freshly brewed coffee and hear soft conversation. There at the breakfast table, speaking quietly with one another, were Dr. Mulligan, Lauren's Therapist, and Ruth.

"Good morning, Lauren," said Ruth, "how did you sleep?"

"Uh, I guess alright, considering. Seemed like I tossed and turned a lot. Oh, to be honest, it was kind of a long night really," Lauren admitted.

"That makes perfect sense Lauren," affirmed Dr. Mulligan, "today is a pivotal day for you and your family. Just remember the things we've talked about and Lauren?"

"Yes mam?"

"Remember to breathe," smiled Dr. Mulligan.

"Yes mam."

"We're going to be right there with you Lauren, the whole time. We won't leave you," added Ruth, "let me pour you some coffee to get your engine running."

Taking the mug of hot coffee from Ruth, Lauren said, "Thank you Mrs. Pierce."

Ruth patted Lauren on the shoulder, "There is a time for everything, and a season for every activity under the heavens Lauren, including this one today. You're gonna be fine."

"Thanks Mrs. Pierce," Lauren looked down at the steaming coffee in her hands, "well, I guess I better go get Lola up," and with that she turned back up the stairs to the attic room she and Lola had been sharing since the night her father had been arrested.

"Alright, but I want the two of you to sit down here at the breakfast table, for just a moment, and at least eat a piece of toast before we leave for the courthouse," said Ruth, "you need to have a little something in your tummy."

"Yes mam."

Lauren entered the attic bedroom, "Lola, wake up," she shook her little sister, "wake up sleepy head."

"I don't want to," Lola covered her head with her pillow.

"I can see that, but we have to get ready."

"What for?"

"You know what for. Today we are going to the courthouse Lola. You remember Dr. Mulligan talking with us about the trial and how we'd be asked questions and all that would happen?"

"Yes, but I don't want to do it. I don't want everyone to stare at you, at me," whined Lola.

"I get it. I understand..." just then there was a knock on the attic door, "come in."

"Morning," greeted Jeannie, "I thought I'd fix Lola's hair if she'll let me."

Lola's face brightened at the prospect and the two of them skipped off, giggling all the way to the bathroom where the hair detangling spritzer was already sitting out on the countertop with rubber bands and hair ribbons.

Lauren sighed, thankful for Jeannie and her help this morning. Jeannie had become a trusted friend, something Lauren had thought she would never have. She knew everything that had happened in Lauren's family and was still steadfast in her support. Lauren sat on the little stool, in front of the mirror of her makeshift dressing table. Actually, a school desk where she applied her makeup each morning. It also served as a study station in the afternoons. Her few cosmetics were in a small, mirrored tray, lined up perfectly, and positioned in the top right corner of the desk. Lauren was very proud of them. Jeannie had made sure she at least had blush, mascara, and lip gloss. Lauren was beginning, ever so slowly, to feel like a regular teenager. Sitting there, she began to brush out her long blond hair. It felt good to work through her hair using deep strokes. For a moment she was lost in the simple pleasure of it all, as she watched her hair become shinier with each pass through. It had been a long time since she'd thought of its beauty or noticed its polish. Instead, for years she'd intentionally kept it dirty and unkept, feeling thoroughly disgusting. She and Lola were safe now, however, so she could chance cleaning up, she could primp, and try to look her best, because no one was going to hurt her. Not anymore, never again. That fact felt good. It felt normal.

The doorbell sounded, and she heard Ruth answer the door downstairs and greet someone. Lauren wondered who would be stopping by the Pierce home so early. Moments later, Ruth was climbing the stairs talking to whomever had been at the front door and stopped outside the attic room and knocked, "Lauren, may we come in?"

"Sure Mrs. Pierce."

Ruth opened the door and stepped aside to let Trish, Lauren's older sister, enter the attic room. Surprised, Lauren rushed into Trish's arms. Trish began to cry and apologize, "I'm so sorry Lauren, I'm so sorry. I should never have left you alone with Dad."

Full of compassion, Lauren responded with comprehension, "You're OK, Trish. I understand. I get it. I'm glad you're here now."

Ruth closed the door quietly to leave the two sisters alone. They sat down together on Lauren's bed, "Pretty nice of the Pierce family to put you and Lola up like this," said Trish.

"They've been great. Couldn't have come this far without them. That's something for you to remember, Trish. I had the Pierce family to help me, and I've had Dr. Mulligan. I've not been alone in all this. You were."

"Thanks sis. Has Mom forgiven you?"

"No. That's been pretty hard. She's still defending him. Denies any of it happened. You'll see, I mean if you decide to go with us to the courthouse. Your support would mean everything to me, but I realize, it's a big step. It's gonna be hard, very public, but it's the only way I could think of to make it stop, to make him stop."

Trish nodded, "It's time I took a stand. Time I was as brave as my little sister. Yes, I'll be there. Of course I will. You have my full support. I'll even testify. Whatever it takes. Together we're gonna be alright sis," she hugged Lauren again.

Just then the attic door slammed open with a bang and Lola sprang into the room pouncing on her two sisters hollering at the top of her lungs, "Group hug, group hug, group hug," the two older girls grabbed little Lola tight and tumbled back into the pillows of the bed they'd been sitting on, laughing together, relishing the pure joy and innocence that embodied their younger sister.